101

Winning Defensive Line Drills

Michael A. Cieri

COACHES CHOICE™

ISBN: 978-1-60679-294-0
Library of Congress Control Number: 2013957532
Cover design: Cheery Sugabo
Book layout: Cheery Sugabo
Chapter page graphic: Vizualbyte/iStock/Thinkstock
Front cover photo: Getty Images

Coaches Choice
P.O. Box 1828
Monterey, CA 93942
www.coacheschoice.com

Dedication

To the memory of my parents—my dad, Anthony "Chickie Boy" Cieri, and my mom, Caroline Cieri—who worked and sacrificed all their lives to give me opportunities they never had. Their life together was one of caring and giving. My dad, who coached youth league basketball and baseball, taught me early that stressing the fundamentals is the key to being a successful coach. And, although mom and dad enjoyed many of the good things in life, especially family and friends, they gave so much more than they took. It is hard to describe how much I miss them and their guidance. I am comforted somewhat in knowing the multitude of lives they affected so positively.

To my best teammates in the world, my children—Carla Nicole Cieri, a physical therapist, and Michael Joseph Cieri, the very promising sports management and construction specialist—who have been and always will be great sources of pride to me. And, to Anna Marie, who spent many lonely days and nights raising these fine two children.

To Joyce Civello, whose patience, understanding, and support make her an incredibly special person to me.

To the many players I had the privilege to coach with over the years and the coaches who were my associates during my career that not only gave me the reason to make my work enjoyable every day, but also very instrumental in making this book possible.

Acknowledgments

To acknowledge all those who have passed on to me the knowledge presented in *101 Winning Defensive Line Drills* and who have helped me formulate the ideas in this book would take a separate chapter. So, I will recognize a few specifically and others in general from all of the clinicians, related professionals, and players I have learned from. I would like to thank the following people.

The five head coaches who hired me over my 42-year career: Rick Giancola, Montclair State University; William Klika, Fairleigh-Dickinson University, Jack Francis, Boonton High School; Mr. Al Nicholas, Mount Olive High School; and Mr. Tom Testa, Belleville High School. Each influenced me significantly and game me the freedom to learn, lead, and thrive professionally.

The assistant football coaches—Billy Walsh, Todd Agresta, Montclair State University; John Pearce, Prairie View A&M University; Ron Cook, Lumberton High School (SC); Sean Cronin, Temple University—for their effort, patience, and sharing to conduct and develop the techniques and drills used in this book. And, the student assistants—Nick Citro, Mike Palazzo, Alex and Vinny Iachetta, Montclair State University—who helped carry out the plan to make the defensive linemen, the "Warriors," an elite defensive unit.

All of the student-athletes, especially Bobby Skinner, former MSU player and a highly regarded prospect on the New York Giants' roster, who are the reason I am in this profession. I hope I've served you as well as you have energized my life. Thanks for the volumes you have taught me. Always remember that you can be a fierce competitor and "Do It Right."

Finally, the staff at Coaches Choice—especially Jim Peterson—for their professionalism in developing a quality product that would benefit players and coaches for years to come.

Contents

Dedication 3
Acknowledgments 4
Preface 6

Chapter 1: Dynamic Warm-Up and Flexibility 7

Chapter 2: Closed and Open Agilities and Footwork
Development vs. the Run 13

Chapter 3: Stance and Starts: Get-Off With Blow
Delivery Development vs. the Run 25

Chapter 4: Blow Delivery: Explosion and Escape
Development vs. the Run 39

Chapter 5: Block Protection Development vs. the Run 51

Chapter 6: Closed and Open Agilities and Footwork
Development vs. the Pass 73

Chapter 7: Stance and Starts: Get-Off Development vs. the Pass 77

Chapter 8: Blow Delivery: Explosion and Escape Development vs. the Pass 89

Chapter 9: Pass Rush Moves: Block Protection Development vs. the Pass 101

Chapter 10: Two- and Three-Man Games and Team Pass Rush:
Block Protection Development vs. the Pass 119

Chapter 11: Tackling, Ball Disruption, and Team Pursuit: Basic Fundamentals
Development for Defensive Linemen 135

About the Author 144

Preface

When it comes to defensive football and the prime directive for that side of the football, it all starts up front, down in the trenches with the hand in the ground. Out of all positions in the game of football, the defensive line is the most technical and physical position to play. The linemen set the tempo and are the foundation of a great defensive team. With defensive line individual, unit, or team practice, there is a level of work that is highly demanded and not negotiated.

This book will provide insight in how to develop your defensive linemen to be more proficient. The primary objective of *101 Winning Defensive Line Drills* is to thoroughly show drills that will develop the fundamentals that are necessary for effective defensive line play regardless of the scheme. The drills and techniques presented will help in building individual player skills quicker and maximizing practice time for your special teams. Individual skill building will lead to group work that starts to build the coordination between players and the scheme. Team success will come from the improvement of individual player skills that will be obtained from these specific drills. These individual drills will make sure that the players understand the techniques, which is essential in the team concept. For defensive linemen to be successful, players must replicate techniques and position fundamentals thousands of times to perfect various techniques against different blocking schemes. Utilizing these simple and specific drills, the defensive linemen will work on actual techniques that will be applied in actual game situations. These drills will enhance blow delivery, working on hands placement on the offensive linemen. The defensive linemen will work in chutes and on sleds to enhance the pad level and playing low so they are doing theses things fundamentally and daily to get them to play with this type of energy and technique.

The focus of *101 Winning Defensive Line Drills* is to work on specific things that are going to happen every time the ball is snapped—like sled work, chutes, aiming points, and targets and hand placement. Working on these skills will increase your team's rate and degree of winning defensive line play.

1

Dynamic Warm-Up
and Flexibility

#1: Dynamic Warm-Up and Flexibility— Linear Movements

Objective: To prepare defensive linemen for movement in a linear direction both forward and backward that allows for increased heart rate, blood flow, muscle temperature, and viscosity of joint fluids, thus allowing for great flexibility and preparing the athlete to move quickly

Equipment Needed: None

Description: Line up defensive linemen on a yard line in groups of four. Have the athletes move through each exercise for a distance of 20 yards. The linear dynamic warm-up exercises targets the flexor, hamstring, glutes, and quadriceps muscle groups. The complete warm-up should be performed within 10 minutes.

- 3/4 sprint: 75 percent effort.
- Ankle hops/jumping jacks: Athletes jump off the balls of their feet, not allowing their heels to contact the ground.
- Walking forward deep lunge with twist: Athletes keep the kneeling knee an inch off the ground, push their hips forward, and rotate their trunk to either side.
- Walking lunge backward with no trunk rotation: Athletes keep the knee an inch off the ground and maintain balance.
- Frankenstein (hamstring kicks): Athletes keep their legs straight and kick the target (a hand).
- Walking quad pull: Athletes pull their leg and opposite arm back to effectively stretch the hip flexors.
- Walking knee hugs: Athletes pull their knee to their chest to stretch the hip extensors (gluteus maximus).
- High knees: Athletes make quick contacts off the ground, not allowing heels to touch.
- Butt kicks: Athletes engage in rapid movement of the feet, allowing the heel of the foot to touch their butt cheek.
- Backpedal: Athletes assume an athletic position, with back flat, looking straight ahead, sitting into position, and staying on the balls of their feet.
- Full sprint: 100 percent effort.

Coaching Point: Don't allow defensive linemen to use extra steps between each repetition in each exercise. This maximizes muscular flexibility and improves mechanics through the neuromuscular system, potentially reducing injury through decreasing reflexive muscle contractions.

#2: Dynamic Warm-Up and Flexibility— Lateral Movements

Objective: To prepare defensive linemen for movement in a lateral direction both forward and backward that allows for increased heart rate, blood flow, muscle temperature, and viscosity of joint fluids, thus allowing for great flexibility preparing the athlete to move quickly

Equipment Needed: None

Description: Line up the defensive linemen on a yard line in groups of four. Have the athletes move through the each exercise for a distance of 20 yards. The lateral dynamic warm-up exercises emphasize the hip abductors and adductors as well as the flexor, hamstring, glutes, and quadriceps muscle groups. The complete warm-up should be done for 10 minutes.

- 3/4 sprint: 75 percent effort.
- Walking lateral shuffles (right and left): Athletes start in a semi-squatting position. Legs are bent to roughly 90 degrees, feet are about shoulder-width apart, and the back is straight while looking directly ahead. They maintain body position, step out to the side far enough so their stationary leg is almost straight. Athletes step up with their stationary leg so they're in the original stance, and repeat.
- Sprinter skips: Using a fast skip to simulate proper sprinting mechanics, athletes lock the elbows at 90 degrees and drive the knee to the belt line with the toe dorsiflexed. With the left knee up and the right arm by the cheek, athletes pause as if taking a picture.
- Sumo squat (forward walk): Athletes go through the full range of motion with a wide stance (outside of shoulders) to stretch groin muscles.
- Spiderman: In a push-up position, athletes bring one foot to their hand, attempting to get their elbow to touch the ankle or the ground, and hold briefly.
- 3/4 sprint: 75 percent effort.
- Carioca (right and left): With quick movement at the hips, athletes' movement should be fluid.
- Lateral shuffle (right and left): Athletes perform just like walking lateral shuffles, but faster; they reach with the front foot, push off the back foot, and don't let their feet come together.
- Side-to-side lunges (right and left): Athletes start in football position with their feet wide apart; slowly, they squat with full range of motion, return back to football position, bring their feet together, and resquat; resuming the football position, they lift the far leg as if going over a fence, and restart the exercise.

- Bounding for distance and height: With two separate movements, athletes use a skipping technique, push off the balls of their feet to create distance, repeat the skip technique, and gain height.
- Full sprint: 100 percent effort.

Coaching Point: Don't allow the defensive linemen to use extra steps between each repetition in each exercise. This approach maximizes muscular flexibility and improves mechanics through the neuromuscular system, potentially reducing injury through decreasing reflexive muscle contractions.

#3: Fast Start Push-Offs—Linear Movement

Objective: To prepare defensive linemen to explode off the ball in a linear direction quickly, launching from the front foot in their three-point stances

Equipment Needed: Ball on a stick

Description: Line up the athletes on a yard line in groups of four. Have the defensive linemen push off their front feet to commence each exercise. The coach starts the drill by moving the ball on a stick. The defensive linemen explode off the ball on the visual key (cadence can be included as a distraction), and sprint for 10 yards.

- Six-point starts: Defensive linemen align in a six-point position. On the "ready" command, the defensive linemen will place one foot slight ahead of the other to assume a right- or left-handed position. On the visual key movement, the defensive linemen push off the toes of the front feet to create forward momentum, sprinting the required 10 yards. Practice both right and left front foot starts.
- Push-up starts: On the "ready" command, the defensive linemen lie prone on the ground face down. On the "up" command, the defensive linemen assume the push-up position. Defensive linemen will place one foot slightly ahead of the other to assume a right- or left-handed position. On the visual key movement, the defensive linemen push off the toes of the front feet to create forward momentum, sprinting the required 10 yards. Practice both right and left front foot starts.
- One-leg balance starts: Defensive linemen assume a three-point stance. On the "up" command, the player raises his back leg. On the visual key movement, the defensive linemen push off the toes of the front feet to create forward momentum by launching off the front foot, sprinting the required 10 yards. Practice both right and left front foot starts.
- Combine stance starts: On the "ready" command, the defensive linemen kneel on one knee on the starting yard line with the other leg's toes aligned on the same line. At the same time, the defensive linemen place their hands on the ground to the side of the knee and toes. On the "up" command, the defensive line raises their hips higher than their shoulders without moving their feet or hands. On the visual key movement, the defensive linemen push off the front foot to create forward momentum by launching off the front foot, sprinting the required 10 yards. Practice both right and left front foot starts.

Coaching Point: The coach must emphasize that the defensive linemen's heels must be off the ground, press hard on their toes, and put weight on the front foot to accelerate the get-off, freeing the back foot to take the first step.

2

Closed and Open Agilities and Footwork Development vs. the Run

#4: Linear Agility—Closed Movements

Objective: To develop the defensive lineman's ability to quickly change directions as he slows down and speeds up through closed agility drills (Closed agility drills are pre-programmed drills done in a predictable and unchanging environment that will improve neuromuscular efficiency.)

Equipment Needed: Agility bags or swim noodles

Description: Arrange five bags or swim noodles one yard apart in a straight line (use sideline markers as a guide). Have the defensive linemen line up at the end of the first bag/swim noodle. Have the athletes commence each drill on the coach's command, sprinting down the line, performing each drill twice (down the line and back). The drills are:

- One in the hole and two in the hole (Diagram A): Straight ahead, one foot in the hole or two feet in the hole—have players finish with a burst.
- Lateral shuffle to the right and left (Diagram B): Players stay facing the coach—have players keep eyes up and pads down.
- Up and back (Diagram C): Players stay facing the coach—have players bend and explode forward and backward.
- Bounding, two feet in the hole (Diagram D): Have players jump straight up, hands in the air.
- Shuffle bags (Diagram E): Players shuffle with hands on bags—have players bend, cut block protection.

Coaching Points:

- Demand perfection by emphasizing maintaining the low pad low (keep the athlete down, with a Z bend in the knees), putting the pedal to the metal to create a level of work that is highly demanding and developing an attitude that the defensive line is "outworking their opponents."
- Finish each repetition with a five-yard burst run at the end of each drill to build that desire to make plays.

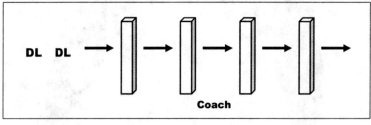

Diagram A

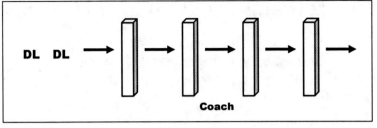

Diagram B

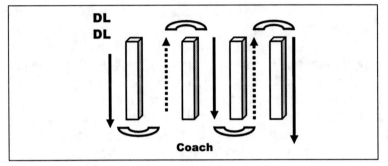

Diagram C

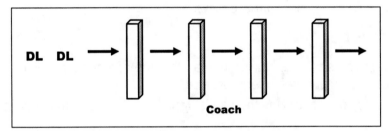

Diagram D

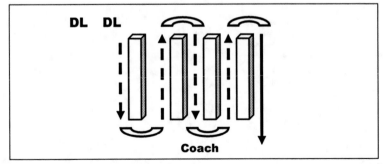

Diagram E

#5: Quick Hands Ladder—Closed Movements

Objective: To develop the defensive lineman's explosive strength in their arms, wrist, and hands and maintain stability in the core and shoulders (Closed agility drills are pre-programmed drills done in a predictable and unchanging environment that will improve neuromuscular efficiency.)

Equipment Needed: Agility ladder

Description: Have the defensive linemen align at the end of the agility ladder in a four-point stance. Defensive linemen will place their hands flat on the ground for each segment of this drill. Have the athletes commence each drill on the coach's command, performing each drill twice (down the line and back). The drills are: one hand in the hole (crawl forward with one hand in each space of the ladder), two hands in each hole (crawl forward with two hands in each space of the ladder), alt punch (alternate hands with one hand between the rungs of the ladder and the other outside the sides of the ladder as the player crawls forward), lateral shuffle to right and left (as player crawls sideways each space between the rungs of the ladder are is filled with one hand), and in and out (players starts with a lateral shuffle with the hands moving simultaneously, one hand will be placed in the ladder, and the other should be outside the ladder in a up-and-down fashion). Finish each repetition with a five-yard burst run at the end of each drill to build that desire to make plays.

Coaching Points:

- This drill stresses to a defensive lineman that the use of his hands is the number-one technique that a defender must acquire.
- This drill is good for working the hands against run blocks or rushing the passer.

#6: Red Hawk Combo Agility—Closed Movements

Objective: To develop the defensive lineman's ability to quickly change directions as he slows down and speeds up through closed agility drills (Closed agility drills are pre-programmed drills done in a predictable and unchanging environment that will improve neuromuscular efficiency.)

Equipment Needed: Agility bags or swim noodles

Description: Arrange five bags or swim noodles one yard apart in a straight line (use sideline markers as a guide). Have the defensive linemen line up at the end of the first bag/swim noodle. Athletes should commence each drill on coach's command with an up-down, followed by a lateral shuffle, ending the drill with the defensive lineman performing a pro agility. Have athletes perform each drill twice (lateral shuffle right and left).

Coaching Points:

- Demand perfection by emphasizing maintaining the low pad low (keep the athlete down, Z bend in the knees), putting the pedal to the metal to create a level of work that is highly demanding and developing an attitude that the defensive line is "outworking their opponents."
- Finish each repetition with a five-yard burst run to end each drill) to build that desire to make plays.

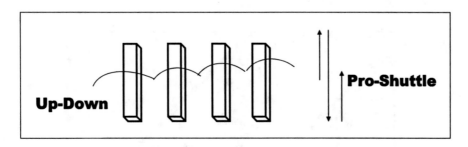

#7: Nebraska Combo Agility—Closed Movements

Objective: To develop the defensive lineman's ability to quickly change directions as they slow down and speed up through closed agility drills (Closed agility drills are pre-programmed drills done in a predictable and unchanging environment that will improve neuromuscular efficiency.)

Equipment Needed: Cones

Description: Arrange the cones according to the diagram. Have the defensive linemen line up at the end of the first cone. On his turn, each defensive lineman, in a three-point stance, gets off low on the visual cue and sprints five yards to the first cone. He plants his outside foot and turns, starting down the first diagonal. On the first diagonal, he can lateral shuffle or perform a carioca. As the defensive lineman reaches the first middle cone, he will get on all fours and crawl through the next four cones (athletes should forward crawl and limit the amount of butt swinging). On the second diagonal, he will repeat the lateral shuffle or carioca. On the final straight-away, he can backpedal or sprint forward. Have each athlete face in on all diagonals. Have the athletes perform each drill twice.

Coaching Point: Demand perfection by emphasizing maintaining the low pad low (keep the athlete down, Z bend in the knees), putting the pedal to the metal to create a level of work that is highly demanding and developing an attitude that the defensive line is "outworking their opponents."

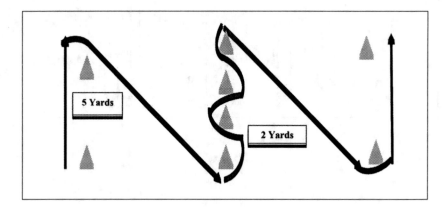

5 Yards

2 Yards

#8: L Cone Agility for the Run—Closed Movements

Objective: To develop the defensive lineman's ability to quickly change directions as they slow down and speed up through closed agility drills (Closed agility drills are pre-programmed drills done in a predictable and unchanging environment that will improve neuromuscular efficiency.)

Equipment Needed: Cones

Description: Arrange cones according to the diagram. Defensive linemen line up at the end of the first cone at the bottom of the T. The defensive lineman, in a three-point stance, gets off low on the visual cue and sprints five yards to the first cone (middle of the T). He touches the line with his hand (facing out away from the middle of the T), plants his downfield foot, and turns back toward the starting line. He will touch the line with the opposite hand and continue back to the middle of the T. Once at the T line, the defensive lineman will turn and sprint under the cone to that side, turn and sprint across the top of the T line to the middle cone. There, he will plant the inside foot on the outside of the cone, dip and rip, and sprint to the start line. Have athletes perform each drill twice to the right and the left.

Coaching Point: Demand perfection by emphasizing maintaining the low pad low (keep the athlete down, Z bend in the knees), putting the pedal to the metal to create a level of work that is highly demanding and developing an attitude that the defensive line is "outworking their opponents."

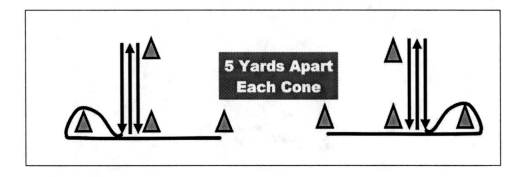

#9: Get-Off and Bend Agility With Angle Tackle—Closed Movements

Objective: To develop the defensive lineman's ability to quickly change directions as they pursue down the line of scrimmage (Closed agility drills are pre-programmed drills done in a predictable and unchanging environment that will improve neuromuscular efficiency.)

Equipment Needed: Hoop, ball on a stick

Description: Arrange the hoop according to the diagram. The defensive lineman lines up in a three-point stance off the end of the hoop at 1 1/2 yards off the ball. With the inside foot back, on the visual cue, he gets off, pushing on his front foot and stepping with his back foot. On the third step (inside foot), he will point the toe inside, bend and rip the inside hand. The defensive lineman will continue flat down the line and perform an angle tackle on the ballcarrier. Have athletes perform each drill twice to the right and the left.

Coaching Point: Demand perfection by emphasizing maintaining the low pad low (keep the athlete down, Z bend in the knees), putting the pedal to the metal to create a level of work that is highly demanding and developing an attitude that the defensive line is "outworking their opponents."

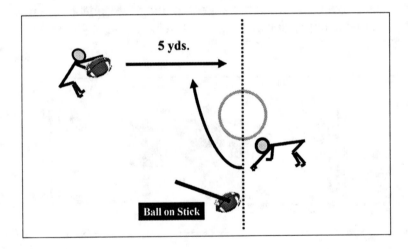

5 yds.

Ball on Stick

#10: Get-Off and Bend Agility
With Retrace—Closed Movements

Objective: To develop the defensive linemen's ability to quickly change direction properly when defending bootlegs, counters, and reverses (Closed agility drills are pre-programmed drills done in a predictable and unchanging environment that will improve neuromuscular efficiency.)

Equipment Needed: Hoop, ball on a stick

Description: Arrange the hoop according to the diagram. The defensive lineman lines up in a three-point stance off the end of the hoop at 1 1/2 yards off the ball. With the inside foot back, on the visual cue, he gets off, pushing on his front foot and stepping with his back foot. On the third step (inside foot), he will point the toe inside, bend and rip the inside hand. The defensive lineman will continue flat down the line as the ballcarrier steps forward. When the ballcarrier runs toward the sideline, the defensive lineman plants his far leg, pivots flat, and runs to parallel to the ballcarrier. The defensive lineman stays down the line and uses an inside-out technique to corral the ballcarrier. Have athletes perform each drill twice to the right and the left.

Coaching Points:

- Demand perfection by emphasizing maintaining the low pad low (keep the athlete down, Z bend in the knees), putting the pedal to the metal to create a level of work that is highly demanding and developing an attitude that the defensive line is "outworking their opponents."
- This drill can be used also when the defensive ends play the quarterback on option or read plays, using the feather-to-pitch technique (sit on the quarterback).

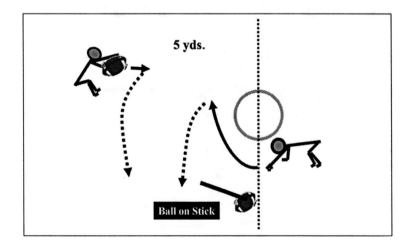

#11: Wave—Open Movements

Objective: To develop the defensive lineman's ability to quickly change directions by improving footwork, body balance, and reaction rate (Open-agility drills basically mimic a closed drill with the addition of a visual or auditory cue to improve cognitive and response-related elements, therefore, increasing defensive lineman to react.)

Equipment Needed: None

Description: Line up the defense lineman as shown and on command have him begin chopping his feet. As the coach points out directions, the player sprints (forward, back left, back right, left, right, front right, front left, etc.), changing direction by pushing off of his outside foot. With one whistle from the coach, the player "breaks down" and chops his feet until a new direction is pointed. On two whistles, he does an up-down and chops his feet until a new direction is pointed.

Coaching Points:

- Demand perfection by emphasizing maintaining the low pad low (keep the athlete down, Z bend in the knees), putting the pedal to the metal to create a level of work that is highly demanding and developing an attitude that the defensive line is "outworking their opponents."
- Finish each drill with a five-yard burst run at the end to build that desire to make plays.
- Open agility drills demand movement, hustle, and reactions under competitive ever-changing conditions.

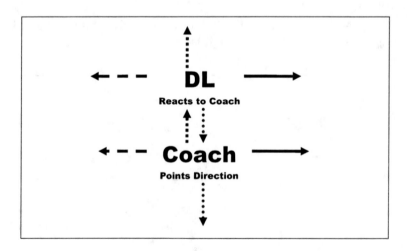

#12: Shuffle Wave—Open Movements

Objective: To develop the defensive lineman's ability to quickly change directions by improving footwork, body balance, and reaction rate (Open-agility drills basically mimic a closed drill with the addition of a visual or auditory cue to improve cognitive and response-related elements, therefore, increasing defensive lineman to react.)

Equipment Needed: Agility bags or swim noodles, cones

Description: Line up the defense linemen in the middle of the bags. On command, have the first defensive lineman begin chopping his feet. As the coach points out directions, the player shuffles to his right or left, changing direction by pushing off of his outside foot. With one whistle from the coach, the player "breaks down" and chops his feet until a new direction is pointed. On two whistles, he does an up-down and chops his feet until a new direction is pointed. When the coach waves the player through to end his turn, the player will sprint down the bag, plant his outside foot, and sprint on an angle toward the cone. To complete the drill, a ball recovery, angle tackle, cut block, or pass rush move on a stand-up dummy can be included.

Coaching Points:

- Demand perfection by emphasizing maintaining the low pad low (keep the athlete down, Z bend in the knees), putting the pedal to the metal to create a level of work that is highly demanding and developing an attitude that the defensive line is "outworking their opponents."
- The downhill sprint at the end of the drill can include angle tackle, a cut block, or playing over the top of an angle block.

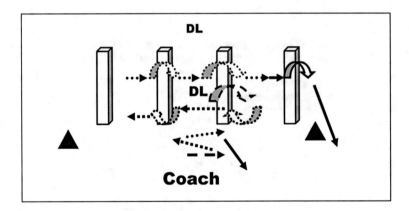

#13: Barrel Review

Objective: To develop the defensive lineman's ability to properly align and carry out their assignments for the defense called based on the various formations of the opponent in a fast tempo drill

Equipment Needed: Five barrels (tied together with rope on handles for spacing), ball on a stick, scout cards (with formations)

Description: Place five barrels as the diagram depicts (hash or middle of the field). Defense gets the call as the offensive personnel is breaking from the huddle after reading the formation card. The defense now makes their strength calls, align, and get ready for the ball to be snapped. On the movement of the visual key (ball on a stick), the defense executes their get-offs using the proper techniques. When the play ends, the defensive players hustle back to their positions, while the second scout squad is reading the next formation card. The next defensive call is made, the second scout breaks the huddle, and all deploy as previously stated. This process goes on for seven plays until the next defense unit performs the drill.

Coaching Points:

- This is an excellent drill to prepare for offenses that use an up-tempo, no-huddle style of play.
- The drill can be devised to do all run formations with matching defenses, passing, blitzing, and unbalanced lines and personnel packages with substitutions.
- Demand perfection by emphasizing proper footwork, pad level and techniques. Have players putting the pedal to the metal to create a level of work that meets the challenge of playing fast.

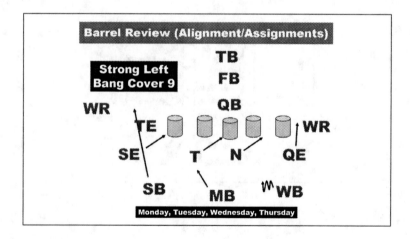

3

Stance and Starts:
Get-Off With Blow Delivery
Development vs. the Run

#14: Power Stance and Get-Off vs. the Run

Objective: To develop the defensive lineman's stance and get-off that allows for accelerating off the blocks, maintaining proper elevation, and gaining the leverage on the blocker by using his hands and feet to defeat the blocker

Equipment Needed: Yard lines, ball on a stick

Description: Have two defensive linemen align on a yard line with one in a right-handed three-point stance and the other in a left-handed three-point stance. On the coach's "set the feet" command, the defensive linemen's front foot needs to be just over the yard line with the heel touching the upside of the line while the back foot's toes should be touching the backside of the line (staggered stance). This will ensure the toe-to-instep relationship of the stance. On the "drop down" command, the defensive linemen will position themselves in a squat (seated) position placing their elbows on their knees. The next command ("finish") will direct the defensive linemen to extend the down hand in front of the player's helmet while the off hand will be placed in the strike position. On the visual key (ball on a stick), the defensive linemen will roll off their power angles and hips, push off the front foot, get the back foot moving forward, and get it on the ground quickly with leading with the hands. The defender should run for three yards before returning to the end of the opposite line.

Coaching Points:

- The coach should emphasize the basic components of sound and effective stance.
  - ✓ When setting the feet, the toes need to be pointed forward and place under the player's armpits.
  - ✓ The up foot needs to be screwed in the ground ready for pushing off it to begin the get-off process.

✓ Placing the elbows on the knees, the defensive lineman allows for the seated squat position that creates the power angles at the hips, knees, and ankles. The heels of the defensive lineman should be off the ground.

✓ When setting the down hand (arm on the side of the foot that is back), the defensive lineman must reach out the arm so that in falls on the ground in front of the facemask. The weight distribution should be on the down hand and front foot more than the back foot. The off hand in aligned off the body in a strike position 6 to 12 inches from the down hand.

• The coach should make sure that defensive lineman is using proper techniques when getting off on the ball.

✓ Hips first: The hips should be rolling forward as the defensive lineman pushes on the front foot to get across the line of scrimmage. This propels the hat and hands to lead the charge.

✓ Flat back: The defensive lineman must maintain a flat back posture upon accelerating forward. The defender's eyes must be focused on the target straight ahead, and his head and shoulder level lower than his opponent's. This allows the defensive linemen to win the battle of power and strength which equates to leverage.

✓ Power step: The back foot steps first with it just clearing the front foot maintaining its plane. This helps get the first step in the ground quickly, which maintains leverage. If overstriding occurred, the blocker has an advantage of power and strength over the defensive lineman. In addition, taking this short first step and getting it on the ground quickly helps the defensive lineman with reacting faster to lateral blocks that the offensive line uses mostly.

✓ Wedge thumbs: When coming out of the stance, the defensive lineman must lead with his hands. The thumbs should be up and touching each other, creating a triangle. The thumbs and hand are positioned directly under the facemask. Don't have the defensive lineman brings his hand back first or begin a running motion. Don't have the defensive lineman shoot his hands (striking the blow/locking out) until the target declares.

#15: Chute Power Stance and Start vs. the Run

Objective: To help the defensive lineman in maintaining a flat back when coming out of his power stance and accelerating off the blocks

Equipment Needed: Chute, yard line, agility bag, sticks (E), ball on a stick

Description: Have two defensive linemen align on a yard line with one in a right-handed three-point stance and the other in a left-handed three-point stance slightly inside the chute. On the ground, place the sticks and an agility bag in front of each of the defensive linemen. On the coach's "set the feet" command, the defensive lineman's front foot needs to be just over the yard line with the heel touching the upside of the line while the back foot's toes should be touching the backside back side of the line (staggered stance). This will ensure the toe-to-instep relationship of the stance. On the "drop down" command, the defensive linemen will position themselves in a squat (seated) position, placing their elbows on their knees. The next command ("finish") will direct the defensive linemen to extend the down hand in front of the player's helmet while the off hand will be placed in the strike position. On the visual key (ball on a stick), the defensive linemen will roll off their power angles and hips, push off the front foot, get the back foot moving forward, and get it on the ground quickly with leading with the hands. The defender should run for three yards before returning to the end of the opposite line.

Coaching Points:

- The coach needs to observe if the defensive lineman touches the top of the chute. The chute helps the defensive lineman to keep a flat back.
- The coach should encourage the defender to take a short first step (power step), set his eyes on the target, and keep his pad level low as he leads with his hands.
- Doing the drill on a yard line aids both coach and player with measuring the power step for overstriding. Overstriding will cause the defensive lineman to rise up and lose his leverage (strength) on the defender.
- The sticks (E) agility bag prevents the defensive lineman from stepping under himself when getting off, which causes him to lose his balance and minimize striking the blow on the blocker.

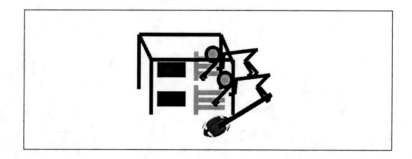

#16: Single-Leg Starts vs. the Run

Objective: To enhance the defensive lineman's ability to push off his front foot and take a proper power step without overstriding

Equipment Needed: Chute, yard line, and ball on a stick

Description: Have two defensive linemen align on a yard line with one in a right-handed three-point stance and the other in a left-handed three-point stance slightly inside the chute. On the coach's "set the feet" command, the defensive linemen's front foot needs to be just over the yard line with the heel touching the upside of the line while the back foot's toes should be touching the backside of the line (staggered stance). This will ensure the toe-to-instep relationship of the stance. On the "drop down" command, the defensive linemen will position themselves in a squat (seated) position, placing their elbows on their knees. The next command ("finish") will direct the defensive linemen to extend the down hand in front of the player's helmet while the off hand will be placed in the strike position. The final command ("lift") will have the defensive lineman lift his back leg off the ground. On the visual key (ball on a stick), the defensive lineman will roll off his power angles and hips, push off the front foot, get the back foot moving forward (leg in the air), and get it on the ground quickly without overstriding. Once the power has landed, the defensive lineman continues to move forward, leading with his hands. The defender should run for three yards before returning to the end of the opposite line.

Coaching Points:

- The coach check to make sure that the front foot toes are screwed in the ground, the heel is in the air, and the defensive lineman is pushing off the front foot. The good indicator is if you have a turf field, the rubber pellets will fly off the back of the push foot.
- The coach needs to observe if the defensive lineman touches the top of the chute. The chute helps the defensive lineman to keep a flat back.
- The coach should encourage the defender to take a short first step (power step), set his eyes on the target, and keep his pad level low as he leads with his hands.
- Doing the drill on a yard line aids both coach and player with measuring the power step for overstriding. Overstriding will cause the defensive lineman to rise up and lose his leverage (strength) on the defender.

#17: Key Read—Get-Off and Redirect vs. the Run

Objective: To help the defensive lineman in getting his first foot on the ground quickly, making an in-flight footwork adjustment, and work down the line flat

Equipment Needed: Chute, yard Line, agility bag, and ball on a stick

Description: Have two defensive linemen align on a yard line with one in a right-handed three-point stance and the other in a left-handed three-point stance under the middle of the chute. On the ground, place an agility bag under each of the defensive linemen. The linemen must have their down hand just in front of the edge of the bag at the end side of the get-off. On the visual key (ball on a stick), the defensive lineman will roll off his power angles and hips, push off the front foot, get the back foot moving forward, and get it on the ground quickly with leading with the hands while reading the coach's hand signal. The coach will point to the left or right with his arms. The defensive lineman will gather his feet with short power steps, plant his foot away for the direction the signal was given, turn his head and shoulders quickly, and sprint down the line. The defender should run for five yards before returning to the end of the opposite line.

Coaching Points:

- The coach should encourage the defender to take a short first step (power step), set his eyes on the target, and keep his pad level low and he leads with his hands.
- Although defensive linemen spend most of their time executing responsibilities with their hands on the ground, this drill is important as they learn how to move as football players in the up, two point, or hitting positions.
- The coach should snap the ball and at the same time use a variety of cadences to simulate the quarterback's action and the snap. Although the cadence has no significance, as far as takeoff is concerned, it does get the defensive lineman accustomed to hearing the snap count as he concentrates on the ball for movement.
- The agility bag prevents the defensive lineman from stepping under himself when getting off, which causes him to lose his balance and minimize striking the blow on the blocker.

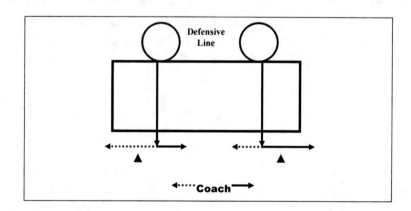

#18: Visual Ball Drop Get-Off—Run Stance

Objective: To develop the defensive lineman's ability to react (get-off) to a visual stimulus

Equipment Needed: Chute, rubber squeeze ball (medium size, textured surface for grip)

Description: Place two or more defensive linemen on one end of the chute. On the opposite side of the chute will be a coach (players) standing sideways approximately three yards away, holding the ball at shoulder level. The defensive linemen will be in a three-point stance. The defensive linemen watch the ball, and when it is dropped they push off their front foot and race to the ball. The defensive linemen will attempt to catch the ball before it hit that ground a second time. The defensive linemen lead with their hands and squeeze the ball with their thumbs up to catch it. This is similar to striking a blocker with proper hand placement. Repeat the drill using the opposite stance.

Coaching Points:

- The coach should check that each player is in a good stance.
- The coach should emphasize that the defensive lineman's first step be quick (when the ball moves), which should enable him to maintain his balance and body control.
- The coach should give feedback to each player regarding the length of the player's first step. If the step is too long, it tends to throw the defender off-balance, causing him to be more susceptible to the thrust of the offensive blocker.

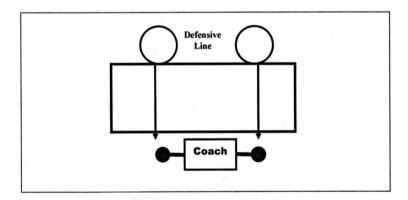

#19: Get-Off and Strike

Objective: To improve the defensive lineman's ability to take an explosive first step and develop a feel of a proper fit of his hands when punching a blocker and then separating from that blocker

Equipment Needed: Chute, half-inch PVC pipes (letter E), shields, ball on a stick

Description: Position a set of two PVC pipes on the ground at the edge of the chute (double-E). Place two defensive linemen at the end of the chute where the pipes are aligned. Have the defensive linemen place their down hand just in front of the top of the first T bar of the E. The coach will stand on the side of the chute with the ball on a stick. On visual key movement (ball on a stick), the defensive linemen push off their front foot and take a short step with the back foot. The defensive linemen use small power steps to drive toward the blocker (shields). Upon reaching the bag, the player should demonstrate the proper technique in shooting the hands to the blocker's chest and running his feet to knock the blocker back. Once the "shoot to fit" is completed, the defensive lineman dips-and-rips to escape the blocker. Repeat the drill using the opposite stance.

Coaching Points:

- The coach should check that each player is in a good stance.
- The coach should emphasize that the defensive lineman's first step be quick (when the ball moves), which should enable him to maintain his balance and body control.
- The sticks keep the defensive linemen from stepping under themselves and helps gauge the length of the player's first step. If the step is too long, it tends to throw the defender off-balance, causing him to be more susceptible to the thrust of the offensive blocker.
- The coach should emphasize the explosive punch of the hands and check to make sure that the hand shield is being driven upward from the punch.

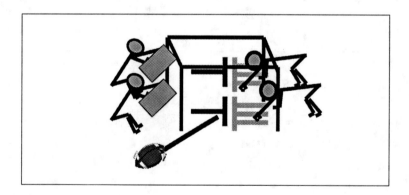

#20: Get-Off and Throw the Hands

Objective: To improve the defensive lineman's technique of throwing his hands into the blocker while maintaining low pad level

Equipment Needed: Chute, half-inch PVC pipes (letter E), tires, ball on a stick

Description: The defensive linemen form two lines at the edge of the chute. Align the double-E pipes as in the get-off and strike drill. Have the defensive linemen place their down hand just in front of the top of the first T bar of the E. The coach will stand on the side of the chute with the ball on a stick. On visual key movement (ball on a stick), the defensive linemen push off their front foot and take a short step with the back foot. The defensive linemen use small power steps to drive toward the tires. Upon reaching the tires, the players should demonstrate the proper technique in shooting the hands, keeping them tight with thumbs up and running the feet to drive the tire off of the line of scrimmage from two yards beyond the chute. Repeat the drill using the opposite stance.

Coaching Points:

- The coach should check that each player is in a good stance.
- The coach should emphasize that the defensive lineman's first step be quick (when the ball moves), which should enable him to maintain his balance and body control.
- The sticks keep the defensive linemen from stepping under themselves and helps gauge the length of the player's first step. If the step is too long, it tends to throw the defender off-balance, causing him to be more susceptible to the thrust of the offensive blocker.
- The coach should emphasize the explosive punch of the hands and locking out on the tires.

#21: Get-Off Slants

Objective: To enhance the defensive lineman's slanting technique and his ability to read his new key

Equipment Needed: Chute, ball on a stick, shields

Description: The defensive linemen form two lines at the corner edge of the chute. One line will be slanting toward the left and the other toward the right. Between the two defensive linemen will be two players holding shields. On the outside of the chute are two players also holding hand shields. Have the defensive linemen place their down hand just in front of the corner pole with the back foot on the side of the outside shield player. A player will stand behind the chute with the ball on a stick. On visual key movement (ball on a stick), the defensive linemen push off their front foot and take a short step with the back foot. As the defensive linemen move, the blocker attacks the defender. As the defensive linemen take a second step and get it on the ground, they shoot their hands into the chest of the blocker. The defensive lineman must rip the backside arm to keep the interior blocker off his body. As the proper fit is occurring, the defensive lineman must churn his feet and push the blocker off the strip. When the defensive line has cleared the board, he separates from the blocker with either a dip-and-rip or swipe technique. Once separated, the defender sprints to execute an angle form tackle on a running back. Have players perform this drill using a right- and left-handed stance.

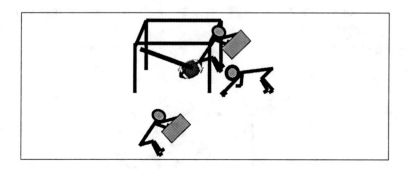

Coaching Points:

- The coach should check that each player is in a good stance.
- The coach should emphasize that the defensive lineman's first step be quick (when the ball moves), take the proper angle, rip on the second step, and make the proper read.
- If the block is a reach-to, the defensive lineman on his third step must plant it firmly in the ground and take the fourth step straight upfield. If the slant is away, the defensive lineman must continue directly down the line flat. If the block is a down block toward the slanter, the defensive lineman must play over the top of the block with his hands. If the blocker sets for pass, the defensive lineman bull rushes the blocker.
- The coach should emphasize the explosive punch of the hands and locking out on the blocker.

#22: Get-Off and Shoot to Fit

Objective: To help the defensive linemen develop a feel of proper fit of his hands when punching to separate from a blocker

Equipment Needed: Six-inch agility bags or rubber strips, shields or stand-up dummy

Description: The defensive linemen form a line at one edge of the strip. A blocker holding a shield assumes a two-point ready stance, straddling the blocking strip. The defensive lineman takes a three-point stance in front of the blocker, maintaining a neutral position between players. On visual key movement (ball on a stick), the defensive lineman pushes off his front foot and takes a short 45-degree angle step with the back foot toward the middle of the blocker (player with the shield on the outside of the chute). The defensive lineman will take a short, 45-degree angle step toward the blocker. As the defensive lineman is moving with his second step, the interior shield player will shoot the back at the back shoulder of the defensive lineman. The defensive lineman must rip the backside arm to keep the interior blocker off his body. By the third step, the defensive lineman must read the block and react appropriately. The blocks that are incorporated in this drill will be: reach to the slant, reach away from the slant, down block to the slant, and a pass set. These blocks are will be performed by the outside shield holder. The defensive lineman should demonstrate the proper reads and accompanying footwork and techniques, such as shooting the hands, keeping them tight with thumbs up, and running the feet to drive the blocker off the line of scrimmage. Have players perform this drill from both sides, slanting right and left.

Coaching Points:

- The coach should check that each player is in a good stance.
- The coach should emphasize that the defensive lineman's first step be quick (when the ball moves), which should enable him to maintain his balance and body control and get the second step on the ground before contact is made.
- The coach needs to encourage proper demeanor throughout the drill. Proper demeanor is a body position in which the defensive lineman has his elbows in, his lower back arched, his feet spread shoulder-width apart, his neck bowed, and his head and eyes up.
- The coach should check the proper technique in shooting the hands into the blocker's chest, the hand placement, and the continuous running of the feet to knock the blocker backward.

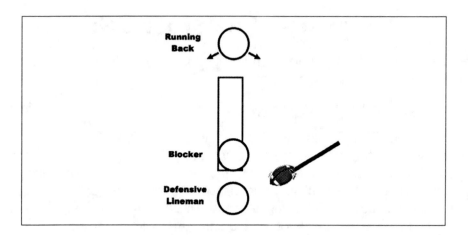

#23: Get-Off Punch and Escape

Objective: To improve the ability of the defensive linemen to incorporate the get-off, the punch, sound and effective footwork, and the proper escape move in defeating a base block

Equipment Needed: Six-inch agility bags or rubber strips, tires, ball on a stick,

Description: Two defensive linemen assume a three-point stance at a line maintaining a neutral zone in front of the blocking strip. Two players with tires in hand are positioned three yards behind the back end of the blocking strip. The tire holders are poised to throw the tire flat (tire treads to make contact with defender) between the defenders knees and thighs. On visual key movement (ball on a stick), the defensive lineman pushing off their front foot accelerates with low pad level toward the tires. When the defensive linemen get to the middle of the strip, the tire throwers release the tires toward the defenders. The defensive lineman must punch the tire, making the tire move backward toward the ballcarrier. This ensures that the defensive lineman shot his hands properly with force and locked out on the blocker (tire). When the tire has been struck and moving backward, the running back starts to run on a predetermined path. The defensive linemen sets his eyes on the ballcarrier, determines what escape technique to use, and then executes that proper technique. If the ballcarrier is one hole away, the defender will use a dip-and-rip escape, while the defender would use a swipe technique if the ballcarrier is two or more holes away. The swipe technique is executed by having the arm and hand to the ballcarrier side remain stationary, while the far hand and arm are moved just under the chin across the blocker's body with the arm and hand ripping down on the blocker's playside arm. The defensive lineman turns parallel to the line of scrimmage and sprints inside out to the ballcarrier. Have player perform this drill from the right and left stances.

Coaching Points:

- The coach should check that each player is in a good stance.
- The coach should emphasize that the defensive lineman's first step be quick (when the ball moves), which should enable him to maintain his balance and body control.
- The coach should check the proper technique in shooting the hands into the tire (blocker's chest), the hand placement, and the continuous running of the feet to knock the tire (blocker) backward.
- The coach can add a tackling component to the drill.
- The coach can have the players throw the tires at the knees to assimilate a cut block. Coach must emphasize the sprawl technique when handling the cut block.

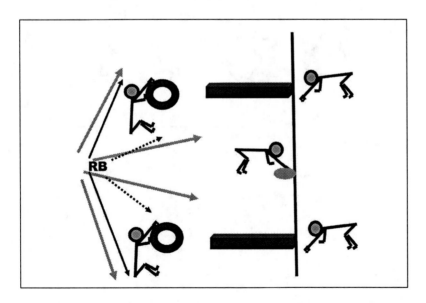

#24: Goal Line Get-Off

Objective: To develop the defensive lineman's ability to explode off the ball and keep the feet moving against a drive block on the goal line

Equipment Needed: Stand-up dummy, ball on a stick

Description: In this drill, a defensive lineman assumes a four-point stance in front of stand-up dummy that is lying at on its side. Insist that a neutral zone is maintained in front of the dummy. On visual key movement (ball on-the stick), the defensive lineman pushes off his front foot and accelerates with low pad level toward the base of the bag. The defensive lineman shoots his hands violently while simultaneously running the feet. The defensive lineman drives the bag three yards straight back off the line of scrimmage.

Coaching Points:

- The coach should check that each player has his hips higher that his back.
- The coach should emphasize that the defensive lineman's first step be quick (when the ball moves), which should enable him to maintain his balance and body control.
- The coach should check the proper technique in shooting the hands into the bag (blocker's chest), the hand placement, and the continuous running of the feet to knock the bag (blocker) backward.
- The coach can add a tackling component to the drill.

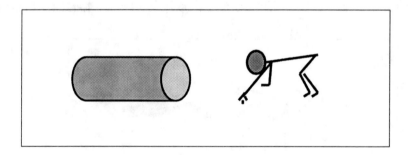

4

Blow Delivery: Explosion and Escape Development vs. the Run

#25: Teaching the Hands—Six-Point Stance

Objective: To improve the ability of the defensive linemen to strike the blow with proper hand placement, rolling the hips to lock out the arms while maintaining a constant head and eye level

Equipment Needed: Shields, seven-man stationary sled or punch board, ball on a stick

Description: In this drill, defensive linemen are in a six-point stance (hands/knees/toes on the ground). The buttocks of the players should be touching their heels (as close as possible). On the visual key movement (ball on -a stick), the defensive lineman explodes out of his stance, rolling the hips and firing arms out as if attacking the offensive lineman. On the punch, the defensive lineman's hands should be placed on the upper outer edge of the numbers on the shield. The palms and heel of the hand should be flat on the shield, with the thumbs up and the forefingers forming a "V" and pointing upward. The punch should terminate with locking out the arms. The arms should remain in this power position until the coach's command to release. Have players repeat this drill three times consecutively.

Coaching Points:

- The player executing this technique should be encouraged to hold the power position with his hands on the bag to really get a feel of performing the skill. This prevents the defensive lineman from slapping the bag.
- The coach should check that all movement of the hands and arms are forward, and there should be no winding up or hitching of the hands.
- The coach should monitor the defensive lineman's head and shoulder level throughout the drill to make sure that the head and shoulder level is lower than the opponent's head and shoulders.
- To determine the distance between the defensive lineman and the shield holder, have the players perform a fit, working the drill backward.

#26: Teaching the Hands—Three-Point Stance

Objective: To improve the ability of the defensive linemen to strike the blow with proper hand placement, rolling the hips to lock out the arms on the second step while maintaining a constant head and eye level

Equipment Needed: Shields, seven-man stationary sled or punch board, ball on a stick

Description: In this drill, defensive linemen are in a three-point stance (hands/knees/ toes on the ground). A neutral zone must be established for the exercise. On the visual key movement (ball on a stick), the defensive lineman explodes out of his three-point stance by pushing off of the front foot and quickly moving his back foot forward. Once the second step contacts the ground, the blow striking the blow, rolling the hips, locking out should be occurring. The drill should finish with an additional two short steps taken, pushing with the toes and having the feet end up on the other side of the line of scrimmage in a slight heel-to-toe stagger. Have players perform this drill from the right and left stance.

Coaching Points:

- The coach must emphasize the importance of attacking the offensive lineman with the defensive lineman's hands. Going after the blocker with the hands allows the defender to attack the blocker on the offensive side of the line of scrimmage. This process of leading with the hands helps to with the battle of the line of scrimmage.
- The coach should monitor the defensive lineman's head and shoulder level throughout the drill to make sure that the head and shoulder level is lower than the opponent's head and shoulders.
- To determine the distance between the defensive lineman and the shield holder, have the players perform a fit, working the drill backward.

#27: Lean and Lock Out—Kneeling

Objective: To help defensive linemen lock out after striking the blow and rolling the hips to shed the blocker and gaining operating space to pursue the ballcarrier and/or rush the passer

Equipment Needed: None

Description: Defensive linemen work as partners. Match the players by weight. The defender is the player who will assume a kneeling position. On the "ready" command, the defender places his hands and arms in the proper position on the number of the chest of the standing player. Once that is done, the standing player leans his body weight onto the defender's hand and arms. The standing player might have to stretch his legs backward to provide the necessary force to make the next action meaningful. On the "up" command, the defender locks out his arms, pushing the standing player back. The defender holds the lockout position until the coach's "ready" command is used. The sequence will be performed three times by each defensive lineman.

Coaching Points:

- The coach must emphasize that the lockout causes the large muscles of the back to be involved in the technique and, therefore, increases the strength or force of the blow.
- The coach must ensure that the defensive lineman is locking out with both arms equally.

#28: Seven-Man Sled Base Block (Stationary)— Swipe Escape

Objective: To improve the ability of the defensive linemen to incorporate the punch, footwork, and swipe escape move in defeating a base block with the ballcarrier two or more holes away

Equipment Needed: Seven-man sled (stationary) or punch board, ball on a stick

Description: Defensive linemen are aligned in a right-handed three-point stance in front of the stationary seven-man sled. On the visual key movement (ball on a stick), the defensive linemen attack the sled from a head-up position. The defensive lineman should explode out of his stance, throw his hand into the sled, and strike the pad with the heels of his hands. His thumbs should be pointing upward. The defender should follow through with a forward snap of his hips and rapid churning movement of his feet. The defensive linemen should drive the sled for three or four steps and then execute the swipe escape technique to the right. The swipe technique is used when the ballcarrier is two or more holes away. The swipe technique is executed by having the arm and hand to the ballcarrier side remain stationary while the far hand and arm are moved just under the chin across the blocker's body with the arm and hand ripping down on the blocker's playside arm. Next, the defensive lineman turns parallel to the line of scrimmage and sprints inside out to the ballcarrier. Have players perform the drill with a left-handed stance and the defensive linemen escaping to the left.

Coaching Points:

- The defender should strike the pad from low to high.
- The defender should form a triangle on the pad as he strikes the pad with his face just above his hands.
- The coach should check that all movement of the hands and arms are forward, and there should be no winding up or hitching of the hands.
- The coach should monitor the defensive lineman's head and shoulder level throughout the drill to make sure that the head and shoulder level is lower than the opponent's head and shoulders.
- To determine the distance between the defensive lineman and the shield holder, have the players perform a fit, working the drill backward.

#29: Seven-Man Sled Base Block (Stationary)– Rip Escape

Objective: To improve the ability of the defensive linemen to incorporate the punch, footwork and rip escape move in defeating a base block with the ballcarrier one hole away

Equipment Needed: Seven-man sled (stationary) or punch board, ball on a stick

Description: Defensive linemen are aligned in a right-handed three-point stance in front of the last pad to the left of the seven-man sled that is stationary. After the player has struck the blow and taken the proper steps, the defensive lineman holds his position with his hands (locks out) on the sled pad, works his feet rapidly, and responds to the hand signal by the coach to escape. The defender will escape to his left. The rip technique is used when the ballcarrier is one or more holes away. The rip technique is executed by having the defensive linemen dipping his far shoulder under the blocker's armpit on the ballcarrier side and stepping with the far leg across the blocker's body and reaching beyond the blocker's leg to the side of the ballcarrier. Have players perform the drill with a left-handed stance and the defensive lineman escaping to the left. An angle tackle, cut block, or down block can be added to finish the drill. Repeat the drill for a left-handed three-point stance in front of the last pad to the right of the seven-man sled that is stationary. The escape will be to the right.

Coaching Point: The coach must encourage the defensive linemen to work directly upfield and not flat as they escape with the rip move.

#30: Seven-Man Sled Down the Line (Stationary)– Rip or Swipe Escape

Objective: To improve the ability of a defensive lineman to deliver a blow against a blocker, pursue a ballcarrier, and make a tackle

Equipment Needed: Seven-man sled (stationary) or punch board, ball on a stick

Description: It is desirable to run this drill on only five pads of the seven-man sled. The defender starts on the third pad from the end of the seven-man sled for a rip escape and on the second pad from the end for a swipe escape. From a three-point stance, on the visual key movement, the player gets off quickly and strikes the pad properly with his hands, locks out, and brings his feet with him. On the "move" command given by the coach, the defensive lineman backs off the pad slightly, working his feet rapidly and then proceeds to the next pad. The defensive lineman resets on the next pad and waits for the visual key before commencing the drill again. The drill moves down the line with first pad being filled with a new lineman after the preceding defender moves on. Once the defensive lineman reaches his final pad, he will execute either a rip or swipe escape technique, depending on how many pads are left on the sled. The defensive line finishes the drill by pursuing according to the escape move. Have the defenders perform the drill again using the other escape technique. Repeat the drill in the opposite direction, utilizing both escapes.

Coaching Point: The coach must emphasize that the defensive lineman works his feet continuously as he strikes, that he locks out as he strikes each pad, and that he keeps his shoulder level down throughout the drill.

#31: Two-Man Sled Attack

Objective: To develop the defensive lineman's ability to throw his hands in an upward thrust

Equipment Needed: Two-man sled, ball on a stick

Description: Two defensive linemen kneel approximately 18 inches away from the pad of the two-man sled. The defensive linemen should sit back on their heels, keep their body erect, and bow their neck so that their head is back. On the visual key movement (ball on a stick), the defensive linemen violently throw their hands into the pads. Initially, the bow is made without hip or leg extension for several repetitions. At this point, the sled can be manned to create weight so it acts stationary. As the drill progresses, the defenders should be required to strike a blow and then follow with an extension of their hips, knocking the sled backward so that the player is able to "lay out" in front of the sled upon finishing the blow delivery. The sled now is unmanned. The defender should immediately recover and present himself ready for another repetition.

Coaching Points:

- When laying out on the blow delivery, the player's body should contact the ground in the following sequence: lower thigh, upper thigh, belt line, navel, and finally the upper abdomen. Observing such a sequence of contact on the ground gives the coach a foolproof read that the athlete is properly developing the desired technique.
- The sled should move upward and outward.
- The players should attack the sled with the heel of their hands, with their thumbs up, and their elbows kept close to the body.

#32: One-Man Sled Base Block—Rip Escape

Objective: To improve the ability of the defensive linemen to incorporate the punch, footwork and rip escape move in defeating a base block with the ballcarrier one hole away

Equipment Needed: One-man sled, ball on a stick

Description: Defensive linemen are aligned in a right-handed three-point stance in front of the one-man sled. On the visual key movement (ball on a stick), the defensive linemen attack the sled from a head-up position. The defensive lineman should explode out of his stance, throw his hand into the sled, and strike the pad with the heels of his hands. His thumbs should be pointing upward. The defender should follow through with a forward snap of his hips and rapid churning movement of his feet. The defensive linemen should drive the sled for three or four steps and then execute a rip escape technique to the right. The rip technique is used when the ballcarrier is one or more holes away. The rip technique is executed by having the defensive lineman dipping his far shoulder under the blocker's armpit on the ballcarrier side and stepping with the far leg across the blocker's body and reaching beyond the blocker's leg to the side of the ballcarrier. Have players perform the drill with a left-handed stance and the defensive linemen escaping to the left. A tackling component can be added to the drill.

Coaching Points:

- The defender should attack the sled with the heels of his hands, with his thumbs up, and his elbows kept close to the body.
- The defender should strike the pad from low to high.
- The defender should demonstrate a good defensive demeanor as he uses small power steps to drive the sled (blocker) straight back.

#33: Maintaining Lockout

Objective: To train the defensive lineman's large muscle in the back to be involved in the locking out process (straightening arms at the elbows), which increases the strength or force of the blow

Equipment Needed: Chute, light tall standing dummy or agility bag, ball on a stick

Description: Defensive linemen are aligned in a right-handed three-point stance in front of the chute man. On the opposite of the chute, approximately two yards off the chute, is a player who is holding a bag. On the visual key movement (ball on a stick), the defensive lineman gets off toward the bag under the chute. Upon reaching the bag, the defensive lineman will the punch the bag, lock out the arms, and run the feet to carry the bag for five yards. The defender will grab the bag on the right edge with one hand on the edge of the bag and the other grabbing the number toward that edge. The bag should be slowly lifted to simulate the concept that all strikes should go from low to high. Have players perform the drill with a left-handed stance and a left edge grab.

Coaching Points:

- The coach must emphasize that the straightening out of the arms at the elbows increases the defender's striking power because if the arms remain bent at the elbows, the strength of the blow is reduced significantly.
- The defender must understand that this straightening or locking out process also serves to provide the defensive player with operating space or separation from the blocker. The defender is, therefore, better able to use his hands to rush the passer or shed the blocker and pursue the ballcarrier.

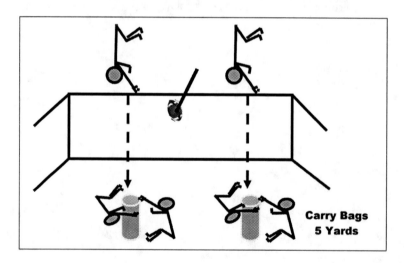

Carry Bags
5 Yards

#34: Two-Point Lockout and Shed

Objective: To improve the defensive lineman's ability in the locking out at the elbows and rolling the hips, which allows for the offensive lineman being driven back

Equipment Needed: Ball on a stick

Description: Defensive lineman begins the drill in a three-point stance, and the offensive blocker lines up with his hands on his knees in a two-point stance. The offensive lineman in the first phase of this drill will be a passive player or the target. On the visual key movement (ball on a stick), the defensive lineman gets off toward the offensive blocker with the proper footwork, striking with the hands on the tips of the numbers of the offensive linemen, driving him back. Once the blow has been delivered, the defensive linemen will lock out the arms and run his feet for two yards and shedding the blocker. The defensive lineman will read the ballcarrier's path to determine if the rip (one hole away) or swipe (two holes away) escapes will be used. Have players perform the drill with a right-handed and left-handed stance.

Coaching Points:

- The drill should progress from little or no resistance from the offensive player to having the offensive lineman coming off the ball from a stance. Again, the velocity with which the offensive lineman comes off the ball should be increased until it simulates an actual 1-on-1 block by the offensive lineman on a running play.
- The coach must emphasize that the defensive lineman maintain his leverage advantage by keeping his shoulder and facemask level lower that that of his opponent throughout the execution of the technique.

#35: Beat the Blocker

Objective: To improve the ability of a defensive lineman to shed the blocker

Equipment Needed: Several cones or agility bags

Description: A narrow rectangle (five yards long and two yards wide) is set off by cones or low profile footwork bags. A defensive lineman who is aligned two yards off the offensive blocker is positioned at one end of the rectangle. The running back is positioned five yards behind the blocker. The blocker fires out when he is ready. On the blocker's movement, the defender takes a proper get-off, shoots his hands into the blocker, runs his feet, and sheds his hands with a rip or shrug escape technique (pull down blocker). The ballcarrier attempts to run through the narrow opening, and the defender makes the hit with a proper tackle. Have players perform the drill with a right-handed and left-handed stance.

Coaching Points:

- No pair of players should be allowed more than two repetitions against each other.
- The coach should direct the drill so that players are evenly matched.
- The drill should emphasize both the need to adhere to proper techniques for shedding the blocker and "competition" between the defenders and the offensive players.

5

Block Protection
Development vs. the Run

#36: Destroy the Reach Block

Objective: To teach the proper push/pull/rip technique by the defensive lineman when the offensive lineman is using a reach block

Equipment Needed: None

Description: A defensive lineman lines up facing an offensive blocker in a two-point stance. Align the players across a yard line. The offensive blocker will perform a reach block. On the blocker's movement, the defender will strike/punch (remember the "V" hand position, wedge thumbs), and proceed to use a push-pull technique (the hand to the side of the reach pushes while the hand away from the reach pulls the offensive lineman). The defensive lineman needs to run the feet and use the push-pull technique to drive the offensive blocker back across the line of scrimmage. The defensive lineman should stay square and not turn his butt outside the blocker. Have players perform the drill with both right- and left-handed reach blocks.

Coaching Points:

- The coach needs to emphasize that the defensive lineman strike the blow with the heels of his hands, drive the blockers upward, and grab cloth just prior to using the push-pull technique. Once the cloth is grabbed, the defensive lineman should not release the hands until the ballcarrier has declared his running path.
- The defensive lineman should work to maintain outside leverage (head just outside the reach side shoulder of the offensive tackle) and keep his shoulders square.
- The defensive lineman should fight down the line until the escape command is given by the coach. The coach with determine the escape move prior to the commencement of the drill. Once the escape has occurred, a form tackle will be performed on a ballcarrier.

#37: In-Flight Adjustment—Advantage

Objective: To teach the proper footwork when defending the reach block by a defensive lineman who has the advantage

Equipment Needed: Swim noodle, shields (if used), ball on a stick

Description: The players are grouped into two lines. A defensive lineman lines up facing a blocker. Align the players across a yard line from each other and establish a neutral zone. Doing the drill on the white border of the sideline can simplify the establishment of the neutral zone. This will help the player and the coach to diagnose if the proper footwork has been utilized. The swim noodles are placed to the right and left of the defender as shown in the diagram. The first noodle must be in the neutral zone. The defensive lineman is in a three-point stance on the edge of the offensive blocker to the side of the reach. The blocker can be holding a shield or in a three-point stance. The offensive blocker will perform a reach block to the right. On movement of the ball, the defender takes his first step straight ahead (power foot) while the blocker is reach blocking. As the power step is being executed, the defensive lineman is reading the block of the offensive lineman. The second step will be the in-flight adjustment step. The defender will point this foot toward the outside playside foot of the blocker while in the air. The noodle will guide the defensive lineman to make the in-flight adjustment before the second step hits the ground. The third step will follow, pointing straight upfield, which helps the square of the shoulders. The strike/punch will occur on this third step. The defensive lineman will proceed to grab the blocker, use the push-pull technique, and run his feet to flatten out the blocker and him drive back across the line of scrimmage. The defensive lineman should stay square and not turn his butt outside the blocker. Have players perform the drill with both right- and left-handed reach blocks.

Coaching Points:

- The coach needs to emphasize that the defensive lineman's eyes should focus on the target to read the block and should not release the hands (grab) on the cloth on the blocker until the ballcarrier has declared his running path.
- The defensive lineman should work to maintain outside leverage (head just outside the reach side shoulder of the offensive tackle) and keep his shoulders square.
- For variety and after the defensive lineman masters the footwork for defeating a reach block, the coach can add an escape (rip, swipe, or shrug).
- The escape techniques are predicated on the number of holes the ballcarrier is away from the defender. If the ballcarrier is one hole away, the rip or shrug technique should be used. If the ballcarrier is two or more holes away, the swipe will be used.

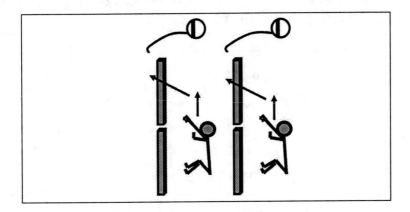

#38: Shuffle to Fit—Disadvantage

Objective: To improve the defensive's lineman's ability to use proper footwork effectively to play over the top of the blocker on reach blocks away (This technique puts the defender at a disadvantage.)

Equipment Needed: Shields (if used), ball on a stick

Description: The players align as if they were performing the in-flight advantage drill. Align the players across a yard line from each other and establish a neutral zone. Doing the drill on the white border of the sideline simplify the establishment of the neutral zone. The defensive lineman is in a three-point stance on the edge of the offensive blocker away from the side of the reach. The blocker can be holding a shield or in a three-point stance. The offensive blocker will perform a reach block opposite. On movement of the ball, the defender takes his first step straight ahead (power foot), while the blocker is reach blocking opposite. As the power step is being executed, the defensive lineman is reading the block of the offensive lineman. Upon reading reach away, the defender plants his second step quickly. The third step will follow pointing straight upfield, which helps square of the shoulders. The strike/punch will occur on this third step. The defensive lineman will proceed to grab the blocker, work his hands across the chest of the blocker while shuffling their feet and using the push-pull technique to flatten out the blocker and him drive back across the line of scrimmage. A swipe technique should be used as this puts the defender two holes away. Have players perform the drill with both right- and left-handed reach blocks.

Coaching Points:

- The coach needs to emphasize that the defensive lineman's eyes should focus on the target to read the block and should not release the hands (grab) on the cloth on the blocker until the ballcarrier has declared his running path.
- The defensive lineman should work across the blocker, keeping his shoulders square while regaining leverage on the blocker.

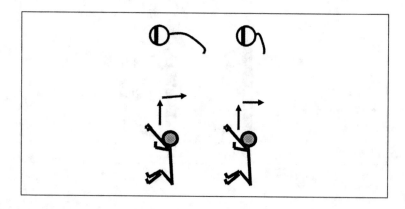

#39: Read and Reach to the Lateral Blocks— Advantage and Disadvantage

Objective: To enhance the ability of a defensive lineman to read and react to reach blocks that are to or away from the defender

Equipment Needed: Chute, ball on a stick

Description: A defensive lineman, who is underneath the chute, lines up facing a blocker, with both players in a three-point stance. Establish a neutral zone to make the drill game day–realistic. The defensive lineman will align on the edge of the offensive blocker. The offensive blocker will perform a reach block to the right or left, according to the coach's command. On movement of the ball, the defender takes his first step straight ahead (power foot) while the blocker is reach blocking. As the power step is being executed, the defensive lineman is reading the block of the offensive lineman. The techniques that were developed in the in-flight adjustment (advantage) and shuffle to fit (disadvantage) drills will be employed starting with the second step. Whether the defender is at an advantage or disadvantage, once the preliminary footwork has been executed, the defensive lineman will grab cloth on the blocker, use the push-pull technique, and run his feet to flatten out the blocker, and him drive back across the line of scrimmage. The defensive lineman should stay square. Have players perform the drill with both right- and left-handed stances and reach blocks to and away.

Coaching Points:

- The coach needs to emphasize that the defensive lineman's eyes should focus on the target to read the block and should not release the hands (grab) on the cloth on the blocker until the ballcarrier has declared his running path.
- For variety and after the defensive lineman masters the footwork for defeating a reach block, the coach can add an escape (rip, swipe, or shrug) and tackling component on a live ballcarrier.
- The escape techniques are predicated on the number of holes the ballcarrier is away from the defender. If the ballcarrier is one hole away, the rip or shrug technique should be used. If the ballcarrier is two or more holes away, the swipe will be used.

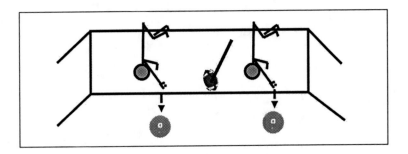

#40: 2-on-2 Read-and-React Live With Escape and Form Tackle vs. Inside Zone With Puncture and/or Cutback

Objective: To develop the defensive linemen's ability to read and react to a lateral block from the advantage or disadvantage position, utilizing the proper escape, pursuit angles, and form tackling

Equipment Needed: Ball on a stick

Description: Align two offensive and defensive players across a yard line from each other five yards apart with an established neutral zone. Doing the drill on the white border of the sideline can simplify the establishment of the neutral zone. This will help the player and the coach to diagnose if the proper footwork has been utilized. Place a ballcarrier seven yards deep between the linemen. The defensive lineman is in a three-point stance on the edge of the offensive blocker, who will also be in a three-point stance. The coach will stand behind the defenders and signal the direction of the reach and the running lane for the ballcarrier. On movement of the ball, the defender takes his first step straight ahead (power foot) while the blocker is reach blocking. After the power step has been executed, the lineman uses the techniques as developed in the in-flight adjustment (advantage) and shuffle to fit (disadvantage) drills. The defensive linemen will strike/punch, proceed to grab the blocker, use the push-pull technique, and run their feet to flatten out the blocker and him drive back across the line of scrimmage. The defensive lineman should stay square and not turn his butt outside the blocker. After the defensive lineman defeats the reach block, the player escapes (rip, swipe, or shrug techniques) and form tackles on a live ballcarrier. Have players perform the drill with both right- and left-handed stances, work on different edges and put the defenders in both the advantage and disadvantage situations.

Coaching Points:

- The coach needs to emphasize that the defensive lineman's eyes should focus on the target (hip of the offensive lineman to shade side) to read the block and should not release the hands (grab) on the cloth on the blocker until the ballcarrier has declared his running path.
- On ball movement, the offensive lineman must attack the defensive lineman's outside shoulder to the side of the reach, and the defender gets off on movement and moves upfield with his feet but throws his hands into the offensive lineman (strikes with the heels of his hands and drives the offensive lineman upward). The defender must maintain hands on the offensive lineman and peek over his outside shoulder to keep leverage and fight down the line to finish with proper escape and then form tackle.
- The escape techniques are predicated on the number of holes the ballcarrier is away from the defender. If the ballcarrier is one hole away, the rip or shrug technique should be used. If the ballcarrier is two or more holes away, the swipe will be used.
- Make the running paths for the ballcarrier simulate the inside zone with or without cutback and stretch plays.

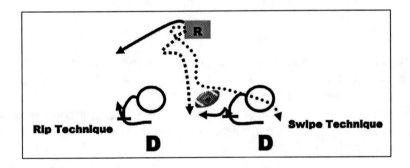

#41: Beat the High Wall Block

Objective: To develop the defensive lineman's (defensive end's) skill in the defeating the high wall block from an outside-shade technique

Equipment Needed: None

Description: A defensive lineman lines up, facing an offensive blocker both in a three-point stance. Align the players across a yard line and establish a neutral zone. The offensive blocker will perform a high wall block. A high wall is a cutoff block usually performed by an offensive tackle on a defensive end on the backside of the play. On the blocker's movement, the defender will push off the upfield foot, take his short power step with his back foot (inside foot), get it on the ground quickly, and read the blocker. On the second step (original front foot), the defender plants his foot, and the third step (original back foot) will be pointed toward the center of the blocker. On the third step, the defensive lineman will strike/punch (remember the "V" hand position, wedge thumbs), and proceed to use a push-pull technique, pressing the upfield shoulder of the blocker flat and playing over the top. The defensive lineman needs to run the feet to help drive the offensive blocker back across the line of scrimmage. The defensive lineman should stay square. Have players perform the drill with both right- and left-handed high wall blocks out of right- and left-handed stances.

Coaching Points:

- The coach needs to emphasize that the defensive lineman must not run around the block. The defensive lineman must continue to work to maintain gain leverage (head just outside) on the upfield shoulder of the offensive tackle and keep his shoulders square as the offensive lineman attempts to cut him off. He should use a press technique and squeeze the gap. Have him maintain leverage on the offensive lineman and grab cloth. Tell him to run his feet.
- The defensive lineman should fight down the line until the escape command is given by the coach. If the play is two holes away, use a swipe escape. If the play is more than two holes away, use a shrug technique.

#42: Reactor

Objective: To improve the ability of a defensive lineman to read and use proper footwork and hand placement when playing a drive block or a down block from an outside shade technique when the play is away

Equipment Needed: Three shields, ball on a stick

Description: Align three offensive blockers (holding shields) in a row about three feet apart across a yard line (or sideline border) with an established a neutral zone. A defensive lineman aligns facing the middle offensive blocker in a three-point stance on an outside shade. The middle shield holder will execute a drive reach block while the wing blockers will execute a down block. The coach will signal which blocker attacks first, second, and third. After each fire out by an offensive blocker, the defensive lineman resets in the original outside shade technique. This ensures that each player will perform the three basic footwork techniques encountered in drive and down blocks. On ball movement, the defender will push off the upfield foot, take his short power step with his back foot (inside foot), get it on the ground quickly, and read the attacking blocker. If it is a drive block, the defender will get his second step on the ground, strike a blow, and run the feet, locking out on the blocker. If the blocker attacks from the wing to the side of the shade the second step (original front foot), the defender plants his foot and the third step (original back foot) will be pointed toward the center of the blocker. On the third step, the defensive lineman will strike/punch (remember the "V" hand position, wedge thumbs), and proceed to use a push-pull technique, pressing the upfield shoulder of the blocker flat and playing over the top. The defensive lineman needs to run the feet to help drive the offensive blocker back across the line of scrimmage. The attack from the wing to the side of the shade alignment simulates the offensive blocker's head in front of the defender's body. If the wing attacks away from the shade alignment (the last option), the defensive lineman will use a backdoor (slingshot technique) play flat down the line. This play simulates the offensive blocker's head downfield on the defender's hip and that playing over the top would be more difficult, forcing the defender to a poor pursuit angle. Have players perform the drill with both right- and left-handed stances.

Coaching Points:

- The coach needs to emphasize that the defensive lineman must take short power step to ensure proper leverage on the block, maintaining explosive punch with the hands and positioning the feet to execute the push-pull technique.
- The drill may be done live with players wearing uppers (shoulder pads and helmets).

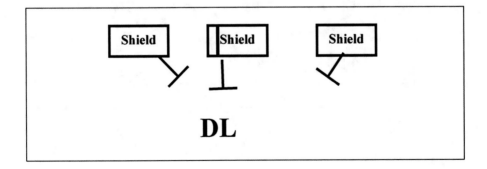

#43: Read and React to the Down Block—Live

Objective: To enhance the ability of a defensive lineman to read and react appropriately to a down block when the play is away

Equipment Needed: None

Description: Two blockers align on the line of scrimmage. A defensive lineman lines up, facing one of the offensive blockers in a three-point stance on a shade alignment. Maintain a neutral zone so that drill simulates game-day procedures. To achieve continuity, the movement key is on the snap count for the two offensive linemen and on the movement of the blockers for the defenders. The blockers execute a typical pull and down block combination. Utilizing proper steps, the defensive lineman reads the flat angle of the blocker and adjusts his path as described in the reactor drill. If the blocker's path crosses (hat in front) the defender's path, the defensive lineman will strike/punch (remember the "V" hand position, wedge thumbs), and proceed to use a push-pull technique, pressing the upfield shoulder of the blocker flat and playing over the top. The defensive lineman needs to run the feet to help drive the offensive blocker back across the line of scrimmage, keeping the shoulders square. This allows for the defender to use a swipe technique to pursue down the line of scrimmage. If the blocker's hat is behind (on the upfield hip of) the defender, then the defender will go back door, using the slingshot technique and work down the line very close to the line of scrimmage. Have players perform the drill with both right- and left-handed stances with the down block coming from the right and left.

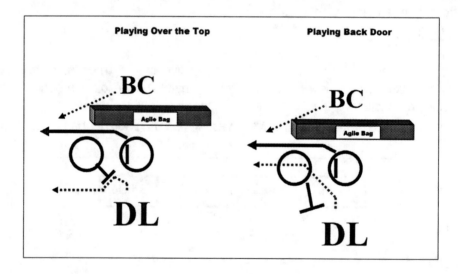

Coaching Points:

- To play over the top of the blocker, the defender needs to control the blocker's shoulders by adjusting the hands across the blocker's chest, using the push-pull technique, flattening out the blocker's shoulders and escaping using a swipe technique. The swipe technique involves taking the hand and arm away from the play and wiping violently with the hand and arm under the nose. The playside hand continues to grab cloth, pressing the shoulder back. On the wipe, the arm and hand will follow through, raking downward to remove blocker's arms while the hips are turning sideways. This should position the body straight down the line so the defender can sprint to the ballcarrier.

- The backdoor (slingshot) technique involves planting the upfield foot, grabbing the far side hip of the blocker with far arm and hand, and ripping the upfield arm and hand along the blocker's backside. This will keep the defensive lineman close to the line of scrimmage in his pursuit to the ballcarrier.

- The drill can also be performed with a tackling component added. This helps with not only with improving proper tackling techniques, but with using the proper escape technique and pursuit angles.

#44: Read and React to the Quick Trap Block—Live

Objective: To enhance the ability of a defensive lineman to read and react appropriately to play the quick trap when the play is to the defender

Equipment Needed: None

Description: The drill involves four players—three offensive players and a defensive lineman, who is aligned in an outside shade on one of the end blockers. The coach, standing behind the defender, signals the offensive lineman to perform either a standard quick trap or an influenced trap on the defender. The defender reads his keys and reacts appropriately. On the standard quick trap, the blocker on whom the defender is aligned blocks down. The defensive lineman squeezes down on the blocker's hips, looking for next threat. Once recognized (puller), the defensive lineman attacks the inside half of the puller (wrong arm technique), eliminating trap and making the ballcarrier bounce outside. On the influence trap blocking scheme, the closest blocker (e.g., the first threat) quick sets and releases outside. The defensive lineman should back inside, go meet the opposite-side puller, and charge into the blocker's inner half (wrong arm technique) to trap the trapper and spill the ballcarrier. Have players perform the drill with both right- and left-handed stances with the trap blocks coming from the right and left.

Coaching Point: The defensive line should attack the inner half of the trapper and not run upfield.

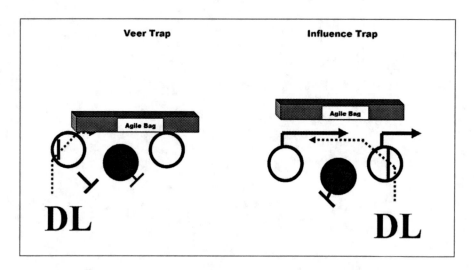

#45: Read the Double-Team—Live

Objective: To improve the ability of a defensive lineman to read the double-team block

Equipment Needed: Seven-man sled (stationary), shields, ball on a stick

Description: The defensive lineman aligns on the end pad of the seven-man sled (stationary) in a three-point outside shade alignment. An offensive blocker with a shield stands alongside the last pad. On ball movement, the defensive lineman fires out into the last pad on the sled (post blocker), and the shield holder jams the bag into 65 percent of the outer half of the defender's body. The defensive lineman shoots his hands to fit into the last pad, runs his feet, and recognizes the double-team. Once the double-team is recognized the defender fights to split the double-team by keeping both his hands on the sled pad, snapping his eyes to pressure (keeping his hat in the crack), keeping his toes, ankles, and hips moving up the field, bending the playside knee (slightly dropping his hip and lowering the playside shoulder), slipping his body between the blockers. This technique prevents the lead blocker from getting a blocking surface on the defensive linemen. Have players perform the drill with both right- and left-handed stances with the double-teams coming from the defender's right and left.

Coaching Points:

- The coach must emphasize that the defender have a great get-off straight upfield, getting his power foot on the ground quickly, shooting his hands explosively to fit into the post blocker (getting his hands on his key), grabbing and maintaining cloth. The defensive lineman must keep his feet moving forward.
- Upon impact from the shield, the defender needs to keep both feet moving forward, jamming his hip into the shield then lowering his hip into the shield to slip the double-team.
- If the defensive lineman feels himself losing ground, he should sink his hips rapidly and violently pull the post blocker down, creating a pile on the line of scrimmage.
- For variety, this drill can be performed live by players wearing full equipment.

#46: Read and Attack the Double-Team—Live

Objective: To improve the ability of a defensive lineman to read the double-team block

Equipment Needed: Ball on a stick

Description: Three blockers align side-by-side, and two ballcarriers are positioned as shown in the diagram. Each blocker assumes a three-point stance. The defensive lineman aligns in a head-up position on the post blocker (middle player). The coach designates two blockers as live, while one of the outside blockers is assigned as a dummy. On ball movement, all three offensive linemen fire off the ball. Two of the offensive linemen form the double-team block. The middle blocker is always live. The defensive lineman takes his power step, gets his second step on the ground quickly, shoots his hands to fit into the post blocker, and recognizes the double-team. When the double-team is recognized, the defensive lineman fights to split the double-team by keeping both his hands on the sled pad, snapping his eyes to pressure (keeping his hat in the crack), keeping his toes, ankles, and hips moving up the field, bending the playside knee (slightly dropping his hip and lowering playside shoulder), slipping his body between blockers. The blocker's feet must actively drive forward. This technique prevents the lead blocker from obtaining a blocking surface on the defender. The defender should use a rip escape to tackle the ballcarrier. The carrier should not run until the defensive lineman is about to split the double-team. Have players perform the drill with both right- and left-handed stances with the double-teams coming from the defender's right and left.

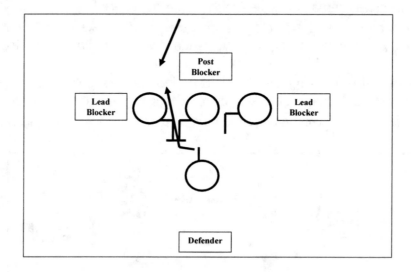

Coaching Points:

- The coach must emphasize that the defender have a great get-off straight upfield, getting his power foot on the ground quickly, shooting his hands explosively to fit into the post blocker (getting his hands on his key), grabbing and maintaining cloth. The defensive lineman must keep his feet moving forward and keep his shoulder square to the line of scrimmage.
- Upon impact from the lead blocker, the defender should jam his hip into the lead, then lower his hip to slip the double-team.
- If the defensive lineman feels himself losing ground, he should sink hips rapidly and violently pull the post blocker down, creating a pile on the line of scrimmage.
- The drill can be run in a controlled manner until the defensive lineman demonstrates an acceptable level of ability at reading the double-team from either direction and performing the technique properly.

#47: Beat the Scoop Block—Live

Objective: To develop the defensive lineman's skill in the defeating the scoop block from an inside or outside shade technique

Equipment Needed: Ball on a stick

Description: Two offensive blockers are aligned as adjacent offensive linemen in cheated splits on a yard line. Each player who is simulating an offensive lineman assumes a three-point stance with his inside arm down. The defensive lineman aligns on an outside shade on the far blocker or an inside shade of the near blocker. The

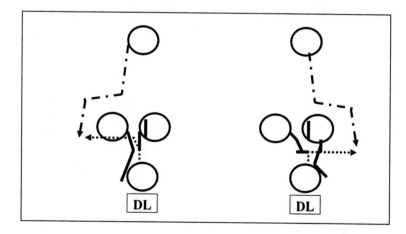

defensive lineman will assume a three-point stance with the hand down (foot back) on the shoulder they are at. On ball movement, the offensive linemen fire off the ball with the blocker in which the defensive lineman is aligned executes a drive reach block while the other blocker executes a scoop block. The scoop block will have the blocker keep his shoulders square and use one arm to secure the defender while the other blocker is trying to take him over. The defensive lineman drives his key back by running his feet, technique (double-team), keeping his hands on the key, snapping eyes to the pressure; he uses the push-pull technique to turn the key blocker's shoulders. The concept is to detain the scoop blocker as long as possible. The defender should split the two blockers and play flat down the line of scrimmage. A ballcarrier can be added to the drill to maintain proper pursuit angles and practice form tackling. The ballcarrier should not run until the defensive lineman is about to split the two blockers. Have players perform the drill with both right- and left-handed stances with the double-teams coming from the defender's right and left.

Coaching Points:

- The coach must emphasize that the defender have a great get-off straight upfield, getting his power foot on the ground quickly, shooting his hands explosively to fit into the post blocker (getting his hands on his key), grabbing and maintaining cloth. The defensive lineman must keep his feet moving forward and keep his shoulder square to the line of scrimmage.
- Upon impact from the scoop blocker, the defender should jam his hip into the lead then lower his hip to slip the scoop combo block.
- The drill can be run in a controlled manner until the defensive lineman demonstrates an acceptable level of ability at reading the double-team from either direction and performing the technique properly.

#48: Wrong Ear (Arm) Kickout/Interior Trapper—Live

Objective: To teach the defensive lineman's (mostly defensive ends) the technique of reading a kickout block or interior trap block using the wrong ear (arm) technique to close the off-tackle hole

Equipment Needed: Ball on a stick, four cones

Description: Four cones are positioned as shown in the diagram. A tight end is positioned at cone #1, while an interior offensive lineman aligned on the line of scrimmage four yards away from the tight end. Placed approximately one yard behind the tight end's inside leg, cone #3 designates the point where the defensive end should be successful in reading either the kickout block from the fullback or a trap block by an interior blocker. Cone #4 is where the fullback will be aligned. The defensive end is aligned in his proper outside shade position on the tight end. Pre-snap the coach will designate who will be blocking the defensive end. The tight end always blocks down. On movement of the ball, the defender drives off his front foot, power steps, shoots his hands into the tight end to gain pad-under-pad leverage. The defensive end should close inside with the tight end, and then attack either the running back or puller. The defensive end should use his outsider shoulder to attack the blocker. The defender makes contact on the upfield outer half of the blocker body by dipping the shoulder and ripping through. This forces the ballcarrier to spill toward the outside to be tackled by the unblocked defender. Have players perform the drill on the right and left sides of the ball.

Coaching Points:

- Although the blocker takes an angular path to the defensive end, the defensive end should attack the blocker on a vertical angle with his shoulders parallel to the line of scrimmage.
- The drill can be run in a controlled manner until the defensive lineman demonstrates an acceptable level of ability at reading the double-team from either direction and performing the technique properly.

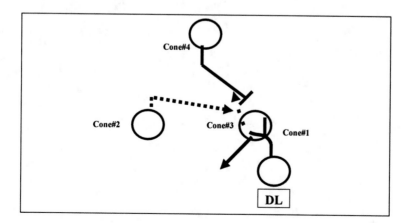

#49: Feather the Quarterback—Live

Objective: To improve the ability of the defensive end to slow-play the quarterback on the lead or speed option

Equipment Needed: Football

Description: A player or coach can act as the quarterback, while a running back takes a position in the backfield as a trail man for the pitch. A defensive end aligns over the tight end that is positioned adjacent to the cone. The defensive end assumes the ready position of a three-point stance in an outside shade on the tight end with his inside foot back. On movement of the offensive unit, the defensive end will push off with his outside, upfield foot and take his first step (power-inside foot), get it on the ground quickly, take a short second step, and react laterally on the third step. When the tight arc releases to the outside, the defensive end must plant his inside foot (third step), keep his shoulders parallel, and open up his outside hip slightly. The defensive end slowly moves to the outside, keep his eyes on the quarterback, never letting himself get farther away from an outstretched arm, nearly touching the quarterback with his fingertips. The player or coach holds the ball in a ready position, to pitch the ball. The coach moves toward the defensive end while the running back maintains the proper pitch relationship. The defensive end responds by shuffling slowly to the outside, learning to keep the proper relationship on the quarterback. The quarterback may either tuck the ball and turn up the field or pitch the ball. If the quarterback keeps the ball, the defensive end should make a high grabbing tackle on him for a short gain. If the quarterback pitches the ball, the defensive end should break to a point that is four or five yards past the line of scrimmage on the defensive side as a cutback pursuit defender. Have players perform the drill on the right and left sides.

Coaching Points:

- When feathering, the defender should keep his outside foot back slightly as he shuffles.
- The feathering defender should extend his inside arm to the quarterback as a gauge to help him maintain his proper cushion.
- An attempt should be made to run the option as fast as possible—an objective that can sometimes be a problem in practice.
- Another dimension is to not use a tight end, but align an offensive tackle that scoops down to the inside like with the A or B read plays.

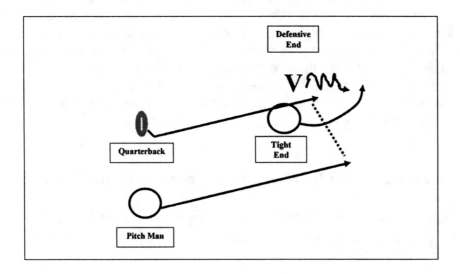

#50: Blocking Scheme Recognition and Reaction—Defensive Ends

Objective: To teach the defensive ends the proper reaction to the various plays that they will encounter

Equipment Needed: Pre-made look cards, ball on a stick

Description: Players align as shown in the diagram. The coach, standing behind the defensive end, holds up a scout card so that the offensive players can see the blocking scheme. As in previous drills, the coach must ensure that there is neutral zone to make the drill more game day–realistic. On ball movement, the offensive players execute the blocking scheme while the defensive end uses proper footwork to get off quickly, read the block pattern, shoot his hands correctly, run his feet, and use appropriate escape techniques. The techniques that the defensive end will utilize have been reviewed in prior technique drills. Each defensive end will perform three or four block reads and react before a new defensive end will perform the drill. Have players perform the drill on the right and left sides.

Coaching Points:

- The proper fundamentals and techniques for delivering a blow and making a tackle should be stressed.
- The game situation should be scripted and explained to all of the participants.
- The drill should be conducted weekly against that week's opponent's blocking scheme tendencies.

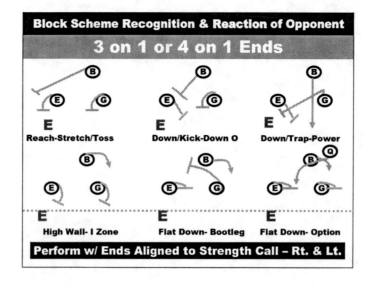

#51: Inside Pods—Defensive Ends

Objective: To teach the interior defensive linemen the proper reaction to the various plays that they will encounter

Equipment Needed: Pre-made look cards, ball on a stick

Description: Players align as shown in the diagram. The coach, standing behind the defensive tackle and noseguard, holds up a scout card so that the offensive players can see the blocking scheme. As in previous drills, the coach must ensure that there is a neutral zone to make the drill more game day–realistic. On ball movement, the offensive players execute the blocking scheme while the defensive tackle and end use proper footwork to get off quickly, read the block pattern, shoot their hands correctly, run their feet, and use appropriate escape techniques. The techniques that the interior defenders will utilize have been reviewed in prior technique drills. Each of the defensive tackles and noseguard will perform three or four blocking schemes and read-and-reacts before a new interior defensive unit will perform the drill. Have players perform the drill with strength calls to the right and left.

Coaching Points:

- The proper fundamentals and techniques for delivering a blow should be stressed.
- The game situation should be scripted and explained to all of the participants.
- The drill should be conducted weekly against that week's opponent's blocking scheme tendencies.

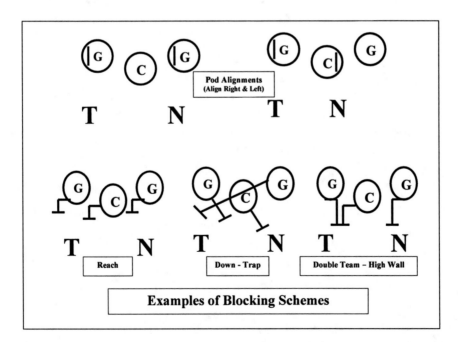

6

Closed and Open
Agilities and Footwork
Development vs. the Pass

#52: Cones

Objective: To improve the ability of a defensive lineman to move quickly, change direction, and adjust his body weight distributed over the balls of the feet to maintain his awareness of how body position and weight distribution factors enhances rushing the passer

Equipment Needed: Cones, hoops, ball on a stick

Description: The cone drills are a series of pass rush agilities. Place the cones and hoops as shown in the diagrams for each drill.

- Linear cones: The defensive lineman will lateral step quickly over each cone. When the defender reaches the last cone, he will step outside the cone and freeze with one foot on the ground and the other in the air. This helps build his lateral stabilizers. On command, the defensive lineman will shuffle back across the cones, perform the freeze again, shuffle back once again, and then run the circle with a dip-and-rip and burst to the quarterback. The defensive lineman should rush to the quarterback's back shoulder and strip the ball with his outside arm while getting his inside arm on his chest to prevent escape.
- L cones: The defensive linemen form a line behind the first cone in a three-point pass rush stance. On ball movement, the defensive lineman sprints five yards to the second cone, where he sinks his body, plants his outside foot, points his toe to the diagonal, and sprints to the third cone. He repeats the sink, plant, and toe movements at the third cone and sprints through the fourth cone.

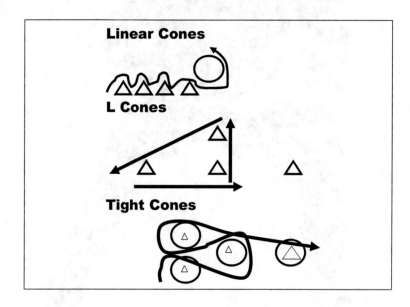

- Tight cones: The defensive end runs the pattern as shown in the diagram. The defensive lineman gets off on the ball movement from a three-point pass rush stance. The defensive lineman dips and rips as he approaches each cone (hoop) and points his toe (bend-point toe drill) to the next cone (hoop). In the flip hips drill, the defensive lineman clubs the back shoulder of a blocker (on air) and flips his hips. Each drill ends with a burst at the last cone, simulating a rush to the quarterback.

Coaching Points:

- The coach must emphasize to the defensive linemen that speed and quickness improves and body balance is maintained when there is good flexion at the ankles, knees, and hips.
- Always perform each drill to the right and left.

#53: Hoops

Objective: To improve the effectiveness of the defensive lineman as a pass rusher, using short, choppy power steps to move his feet quickly and changing direction by pointing his toe to the passer

Equipment Needed: Hoops (8 to 10 feet in diameter), ball on a stick

Description: The hoops drills are a series of pass rush agilities. Place the hoop(s) as shown in the diagrams for each drill. Perform all drills to the right and left with the defensive lineman using a proper edge stance. Maintain a neutral zone.

- Half hoop: The defensive lineman aligns on the edge of the hoop in a three-point stance. On ball movement, the defensive lineman gets off with a low pad level (ankles, knees, and hips bent), dropping his inside arm and touching the inside of the hoop as he moves around the backside of the hoop. The defensive lineman must point his inside toe toward the hoop and lean in. Once the defensive lineman clears the hoop, he will rip through will the inside arm, picking up a towel.
- Full hoop: Three exercises encompass the full hoop drills. The defensive lineman aligns on the edge of the hoop in a three-point stance. On ball movement, the defensive lineman gets off with a low pad level (ankles, knees, and hips bent). In exercise one, the defensive lineman will sprint around the hoop, lean in, and dip, touching the hoop with inside hand. The lineman will finish the drill with a burst as if he is rushing the quarterback. With exercise two, the defensive lineman sprints off the ball, runs the hoop, leaning in as he continuously rips with his inside arm and hand. The rip must be violent and full range. An extra player is needed for exercise three. An offensive blocker will be added inside the hoop. As the defensive lineman runs the hoop, the blocker will jam his hands on the pass rush, simulating

an offensive lineman executing pass protection. The blocker will continue around the hoop with the defender. The defensive lineman will use the techniques worked on in exercises one and two to pass rush and finish.

- Two hoops: This drill will incorporate the use of two hoops. Align two defensive linemen on one hoop at the 45 and hour marks. This drill is a figure-eight chase drill. On the start command, the two linemen get off with low pad level, sprint around the hoops in a figure-eight pattern with one lineman chasing the other. Both players, whether touched from behind or not, sprint with a burst to a tall bag, where they will conduct a proper strip of the ball technique on the quarterback.

Coaching Point: The coach must emphasize to the defensive linemen that speed and quickness improves and body balance is maintained when there is good flexion at the ankles, knees, and hips.

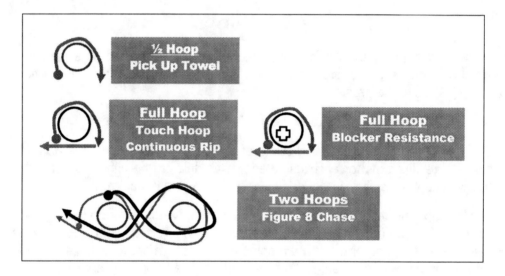

7

Stance and Starts: Get-Off Development vs. the Pass

#54: Visual Key Get-Off

Objective: To improve the ability of a pass rushing defensive lineman to react to a visual stimulus and take an explosive first step

Equipment Needed: Rubber squeeze ball (medium size, textured surface for grip), chute (if used)

Description: Have two defensive linemen align on a yard line with one in a right-handed three-point stance and the other in a left-handed three-point stance. The drill can be performed under a chute. On the coach's "set the feet" command, the defensive linemen's front foot needs to be just over the yard line with the heel touching the upside of the line while the back foot's toes should be slightly more than a heel-toe stagger. The position of the back foot is used only pass rush situations. On the "drop down" command, the defensive linemen will position themselves in a squat (seated) position, placing their elbows on their knees. The next command ("finish") will direct the defensive linemen to extend the down hand in front of the player's helmet while the offhand will be placed in the strike position. The coach stands four yards away from the defenders with a medium size, textured rubber squeeze ball in each arm. After the coach gives the stance commands, he raises his arms to shoulder level. The defensive linemen should be focused on the balls. When the balls are released simultaneously (the visual key), the defensive linemen will roll off their power angles and hips, push off the front foot, get the back foot moving forward, and get it on the ground quickly with leading with the hands. In this pass rush stance, the first step is slightly longer than getting off in on a run down. The defensive lineman will lead with his hands and catch the ball with his hands up (wedge thumbs). The defender should run for three yards before returning to the ball to the coach and going to the end of the opposite line.

Coaching Points:

- The coach should check the stance of each defensive lineman.
- The coach should give feedback to each player regarding the length of the player's first step. If the step in too long, it tends to throw the defender off-balance, raising his chest up and making him more susceptible to the thrust of the offensive blocker when he uses his hands to jam the defender.

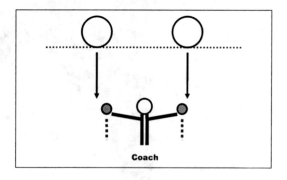

- The coach must emphasize on all pass rush drill the five musts for a sound and effective pass rush: get off, close, escape, finish, burst.

#55: Sic 'Em

Objective: To develop the ability of a defensive lineman to improve his get-off and his first step on a pass rush, and to enhance the foot speed of a pass rushing defensive lineman who plays on the edge

Equipment Needed: Ball on a stick

Description: The coach positions a player (who serves as the rabbit) two yards off a yard line. He also positions a pass rushing defensive lineman on the same yard so that he is facing the "rabbit." On ball movement, the player acting as the rabbit backpedals as quickly as he can. The defensive lineman, using a pass rush stance and get-off, attempts to touch the rabbit before the two of them reach the next five-yard-line marker. The pair should repeat this maneuver a predetermined number of times, and then switch roles. Have the defensive lineman perform this drill using right- and left-handed stances.

Coaching Points:

- Each defensive lineman should move on ball movement.
- If the defensive lineman can touch the rabbit in this drill before the rabbit reaches the five-yard marker, he will discover the likelihood that, in a game situation, the offensive lineman will not be able to block his speed rush.

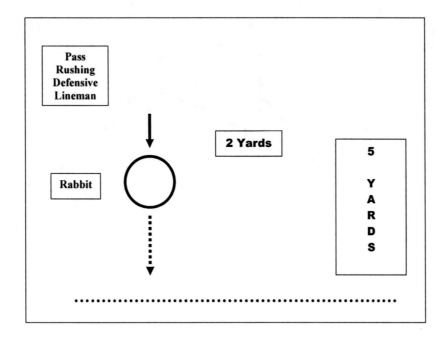

#56: Ball on a Cone Get-Off—Two-Man Competition

Objective: To enhance the ability of a defensive lineman to pass rush by improving his get-off and his first step, and working under the blocker's shoulder pads

Equipment Needed: Ball on a stick, chute, orange cone (standard size), tennis ball

Description: The coach places the edge of a chute on a yard-line marker. On the outside of the chute, the coach will place an orange cone with a tennis ball resting on the top of the cone. The placement of the cone will be four yards beyond the chute in the middle. Two defensive linemen align in a three-point stance (right-handed and left-handed) under the chute. On movement of the ball, the defensive linemen (using a pass rush stance) take off with the proper footwork and sprint to the cone. The defensive linemen are competing to get to the ball first. As they approach the ball on the cone, the defensive linemen will dip-and-rip, grabbing the ball and finishing the rip technique. The players should burst for an additional five yards. Each player should perform this drill from a right- and left-handed stance. The coach can pair off the defensive linemen and have an elimination contest to find the fastest get-off.

Coaching Point: Each defensive lineman should move on ball movement, push off the front foot, take a slight elongated step, and maintain low pad level.

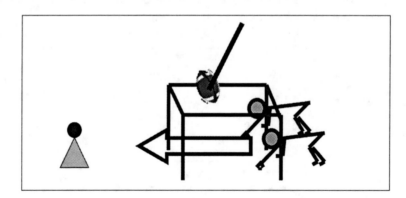

#57: Tag Get-Off

Objective: To develop the ability of a defensive lineman to improve his get-off, aiming point, pad level, and bending toward the quarterback in pass rush

Equipment Needed: Cones, tennis ball or towels, ball on a stick

Description: Establish a line of scrimmage as a starting point for the defenders. Place each cone four yards behind the line of scrimmage. Place each towel or tennis ball slightly behind and to the right (left) of each cone. Each defensive lineman will line up at the line of scrimmage to the left (right) of the cone in a three-point outside edge stance. Maintain a neutral zone between the offensive blocker (who is set off the line) and the defender. The offensive lineman assumes a two-point football pass protection ready position with his head back and his knees bent. On ball movement, the offensive blocker will kick step back or backpedal toward the cone as fast as he can. The defender must get off quickly with low pad level and beat the blocker to the cone. The defender must be able to dip his inside shoulder, rip, and pick up the tennis ball or towel behind the cone. Two repetitions to the left side and then right side should be performed.

Coaching Point: The coach can break this drill into the following stages:
- Stage #1: Just use the cones and towels (tennis ball), no blockers
- Stage #2: Use cones, towels (tennis ball), blockers
- Stage #3: Just have the blocker go straight back

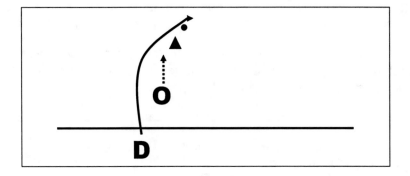

#58: Get Off With Redirect

Objective: To develop the ability of a defensive lineman to improve his get-off, move, and change direction quickly after reading and reacting to a visual stimulus

Equipment Needed: Ball on a stick, chute, football

Description: The coach places the edge of a chute on a yard-line marker. The coach stands with a football five yards from the edge of the chute. Two players will be aligned outside the chute, simulating two wide receivers. Two defensive linemen align in a three-point stance (right-handed and left-handed) under the chute. The coach is responsible for using the football to signal the defenders as to what type of play is occurring. If the coach points the ball to the right or left belt high, the defensive lineman will plant his outside foot and work immediately down the line. This stimulates a run. When the coach raises the ball up, the defensive linemen will burst upfield, stimulating a pass rush on a dropback pass. When the coach raises the ball and drops the ball down quickly, the defensive linemen react to a draw by stopping their rush and sprinting back to the line of scrimmage and back through the chute. If the coach raises the ball and throws it out to one of the wide receivers, the defensive ends will get back to where they came from and pursue. This means that the defenders will sprint back to the line of scrimmage and then take the proper cut-off pursuit angle. The action stimulates a rocket, quick screen. On movement of the ball, the defensive linemen will push off of their front foot, take a quick first step, explode out of their stance, and sprint through the chute. The defensive linemen focus on the coach to read and react to the coach's visual stimulus. Each player should perform this drill from a right- and left-handed stance. The coach must have the players move to their right and left.

Coaching Point: The coach must emphasize to the defensive lineman to plant his upfield (outside) foot, which helps, equalizing the pressure on both feet, to push off and change direction quickly and efficiently.

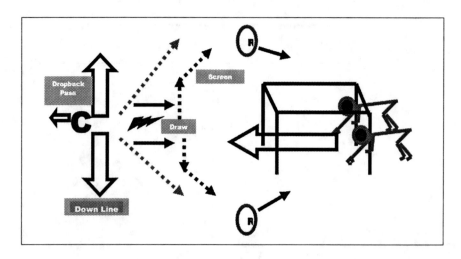

#59: Racing to the Passer—Two-Man Competition

Objective: To improve the defensive lineman's ability to race to the set point, closing the gap, escaping the blocker, and accelerating to the quarterback

Equipment Needed: Ball on a stick, cones, tall bags

Description: Two defensive linemen align on a yard-line marker. A cones are placed four yards off the line of scrimmage, not including the neutral zone to the inside of each defender. Large stand-up dummies are placed at seven to eight yards off the line of scrimmage to the inside of the defensive linemen simulating the position of a pocket passer. The defensive linemen align in a three-point pass rush stance. On the snap of the ball, the defensive linemen get off quickly and sprint to the cone, maintaining low pad level and moving straight ahead. On approach to the cone, each defender must plant his outside foot (without widening the plant foot), point his toe to the tall bag, dip and rip around the cone. The defensive lineman bursts to the tall bag and executes a reach-around (stripping the ball from the back arm of the quarterback) technique on the ball. The defensive linemen gather themselves after the reach-around technique, plant the upfield foot, and sprint straight ahead to the original line of scrimmage. The coach can run the drill like a tournament to an eventual winner. Have players perform the drill both to the right and left with right- and left-handed stances.

Coaching Points:

- This drill teaches, simulates, and emphasizes—without contact—that speed and quickness, the ability to maintain pad under pad leverage, and maintaining body position and balance while moving quickly to the quarterback are keys to be a good passer rusher.
- For variation, the coach can add a blocker at the line of scrimmage, who kick slides straight back and jams the defensive pass rusher. The defensive linemen use hand parries to knock down the offensive blocker's arms and hands.

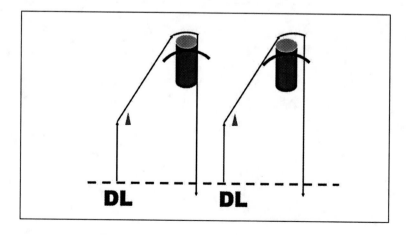

#60: Crazy Ball Get-Off

Objective: To improve the timing of the defensive lineman to jump and alter a pass or enhance the techniques to recover a loose football

Equipment Needed: Rubber squeeze ball (medium size, flexible grip, can bounce)

Description: Two defensive linemen align in the chute. The coach, with ball in hand, will be 10 yards from the chute. On the snap, the defensive linemen get off under the chute and sprint through it. The coach simultaneously releases the ball, bouncing it high (simulates getting hands up on pass) or low to recover a ball on the ground. Both players are competing for the ball. If the ball is high in the air, the defensive linemen will jump to the highest point and grab the ball. If the ball is on the ground, the defensive linemen will either scoop and score or recover the ball and protect it by going to the fetal position. Perform the drill both to the right and left with right- and left-handed stances.

Coaching Points:

- This drill teaches, simulates, and emphasizes—without contact—the fundamentals of a defensive lineman disrupting the pass offense's rhythm and coordinated effort to throw the ball, as opposed to just sacking the quarterback.
- The defensive linemen should understand that the ball can be deflected for a possible interception or their attempts to bat the pass can distract the quarterback's visible passing lane, giving more time for the coverage to converge on the ball.

#61: Scramble Contain/Rocket Screen Pursuit

Objective: To improve the ability of defensive linemen to execute a coordinated pass rush when herding in a scrambling quarterback and/or reacting to a rocket screen and pursuing the wide receiver

Equipment Needed: Football, ball on a stick

Description: Align two defensive linemen on a yard-line marker. A quarterback, in a shotgun position, aligns seven to eight yards in the backfield between the two defenders. To the right and left, place receivers wide to simulate the screen pass to them. The coach will stand behind the defensive linemen and signal the offensive players if the quarterback will take a two-step drop and then scramble or throw the ball to the wide receiver. On ball movement, the defensive linemen will get off and sprint up-field. At the four-yard mark, the defensive linemen will read and react to the quarterback, who has committed to the play. If the quarterback is scrambling and between the defenders, the defenders will slowly attack the pass, squeezing him with outside inside leverage. If the passer escapes the pocket, the defender closest to the scrambler will use inside-out leverage, while the other defender will piggyback the first defender. If the quarterback throws the ball to the wide receiver, the wideout will run back toward the center. The defenders will sprint toward the line of scrimmage (go back to where they came from) and pursue the wideout from an inside-out angle with proper spacing between them. Perform the drill both to the right and left with right- and left-handed stances.

Coaching Points:

- This drill teaches, simulates, and emphasizes—with limited contact—containing a quarterback who likes to run wide, sprints out, or throws numerous quick screens to the wideouts by changing directions and maintaining leverage on the passer.
- An optional component of this drill is that offensive linemen, an extra wide receiver as a blocker, and/or running backs can be added to simulate game-day actions. The defensive linemen can use pass rush moves on the offensive linemen, the running back can use cut blocks, and the wide receiver can block the pursuers.

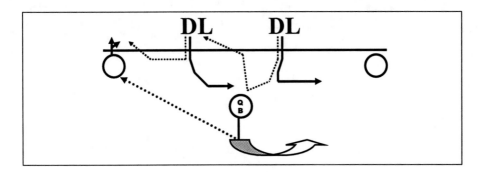

#62: Pass Knockdown

Objective: To improve the ability of a pass rushing defensive lineman to bat down passes

Equipment Needed: Football

Description: A defensive lineman aligns in a three-point outside shade stance on a yard-line marker, maintaining a neutral zone. On offensive a lineman will be positioned opposite the defender in a two- or three-point stance, a running back positioned inside the offensive lineman, and a quarterback aligned inside the running back five to six yards deep with ball in hand. The coach will stand behind the defensive lineman and signal to the offensive players, who will be blocking, and to the quarterback on what type of drop to take. The ball will be released by the quarterback, depending on the drop. If it is a three-step drop, the quarterback will hold the ball for 1.5 seconds (or a "one-Mississippi" count) or a five-step drop in which the ball will be held for 3.5 seconds (or a "two-Mississippi" count). On the snap of the ball, the defensive line will get off quickly, reading and reacting to the blocker and the passer. The defensive line will use a bull rush technique on either the lineman or running back blockers. The defender will use appropriate bat-the-ball techniques. This drill should be performed to the right and left and with both a left- and right-handed quarterback.

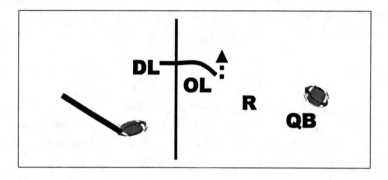

Coaching Points:

- The rules for altering or batting a pass always commence with the defensive lineman learning to raise the opposite arm and hand straight up when trying to deflect the pass.
- When the defensive lineman is fitted on a blocker, the defender should not jump on the throw. This technique helps prevent the defensive lineman from being pulled down or cut blocked by the blocker. It also allows the defensive lineman to keep the opposite arm and hand straight up to either bat the ball or alter the vision of the quarterback.
- If there is an offensive blocker between the defensive lineman and the quarterback, and the defender is not engaged, the defensive lineman can jump and use the proper arm and hand to deflect the ball.
- If the defensive lineman has a clear path to the quarterback, and is one or two arm lengths from the quarterback, the defensive lineman must make a decision to jump if the pass is eminent, or continue to stay on his feet and attack the quarterback or shimmy in front of the passer. If the passer is known to pull the ball down and step up or scramble, the defensive lineman might have to shimmy, regroup in order to contain the quarterback, jump to bat the ball, alter the quarterback's mechanics, or go for a ball strip or sack.

8

Blow Delivery: Explosion and Escape Development vs. the Pass

#63: Gauntlet Pass Rush

Objective: To develop the pass rushing defensive lineman's ability to violently swat his hands and arms while increasing the velocity of his footwork and opening the hips

Equipment Needed: Vertical standing (weighted bottoms) bags or kickboxing training bags (bags that will not mover or tip over), quarterback bag (with arms), ball on a stick

Description: Place three bags in a single-file line five yards apart on a yard-line marker. A fourth bag is place to the right or left of the last bag in line approximately five yards deep and five yards to the inside. Defensive linemen will form a line behind the first bag, which is opposite the last bag, simulating the quarterback. Each defensive lineman will align in a three-point outside shade stance (opposite shade of quarterback bag) on a yard-line marker, maintaining a neutral zone. The defensive lineman, on the snap, gets off the ball quickly and executes a pass rush technique. A pass rush stance and elongated first step is used to close the gap to the bag. The same arm/same foot principle must be used to make the pass rush more effective. Once the move is complete, the defensive lineman approaches the next bag, begins the drill with on the opposite side, and repeats the process. The coach can make it a more rapid-fire drill by having the defensive lineman begin in a two-point stance and make the drill continuous without stopping at each bag. Once the last bag is complete, the defensive lineman points his toe toward the quarterback (bag or coach with ball in hand), rip escapes, and bursts to the bag to perform a proper strip-the-ball technique. Each pass rush technique should be performed to the right and left.

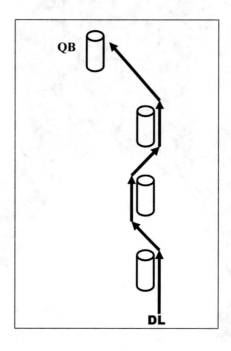

- Big rip: The aiming point that the defensive linemen must strive for is inside the rib cage of the offensive lineman for this inside hand, inside foot technique. It is important that the rip is "wound up." The defender wants to drive the arm slightly back before he uses the rip working forward. The defensive lineman must finish with the bicep of the ripping arm at the ear hole of the helmet. The footwork is tied together, once again, utilizing what is phrased as a drive step. The drive step is a slightly over strided first step that gets the pass rusher's hips working forward giving power to the rip.
- Club flip: The defensive lineman will be using an outside hand and foot technique on this move. The defender must drive to get even with the outside of the bag. The defensive lineman will swat violently the bag with an open hand and simultaneously open (flip the hips) to clear the bag (blocker). The defender will point his toe to the inside, rip escape, and burst to the quarterback. If the defensive lineman attempts to club too early or doesn't open his hip to be totally sideways to the blocker, the pass rush will be negated.
- Chop hoop: The defensive lineman will use an inside arm chop movement. Initially, the arm turns into what is called the "ice pick and dent" arm, coming over the top continuing in a violent, downward motion on the blocker's arm near the wrist. The same foot that steps with this hand should always land with a bent knee so as to avoid falling over. Once the chop has occurred and the blocker's arm is displaced toward the center of the blocker's body, the defender points his inside foot toward the quarterback and uses a dip-and-rip escape.
- Jab olé: This is a counter move, usually used by interior defensive lineman. This move is effective to get the offensive blocker to move his power foot (inside), exposing the outside rush lane. The defensive lineman aligns in a three-point outside shade stance. On ball movement, the defender moves his inside foot (back foot) toward the far leg of the blocker as if he was slanting. The offensive lineman moves his feet to the inside to cut off the slanter. On his second step (front foot), the defensive lineman steps straight up the field. The defender uses a big rip, club flip, or chop hoop pass rush technique with a dip-and-rip escape. If the blocker doesn't move, the defensive lineman will just bull rush down the middle of the offensive blocker.
- Turkey club: A defensive linemen will switch his stance for this counter move, usually used by interior defensive lineman. The defender will use an edge stance with the outside foot back, and get off the ball quickly with that slightly elongated power step. This step, along with body demeanor, should dictate to the blocker that the defensive lineman is executing an outside speed rush. The blocker should respond by kick-sliding slightly to the outside, leaving an inside track to pass rush and destroying the offensive lineman's power foot to recover. The outside step must be planted in the ground, like a T-step that a defensive back will use. This is to propel the defender's body to shuffle with very short choppy steps (shimmy) in front of the blocker's body and perform a club flip on the other side of the blocker's body. The defensive lineman will use a dip-and-rip escape and accelerate to the quarterback.

Coaching Points:

- The coach must emphasize to the defensive lineman that the most crucial technique is that the pass rusher's hands and feet are tied together, working as one when the move is in progress. Whatever he does with your right hand, he must step with his right foot. Any techniques with the left hand must correspond with a step by the left foot. This must be taught because it is opposite of how the human body normally operates. When people run or walk, the body works in a plane of motion that operates under the principle of opposite hand/opposite foot. Pass rush is same hand/same foot, just like a marionette puppet.
- For variety, the bags can be replaced with live offensive linemen, who can kick slide straight back and apply light pressure punches to simulate a more realistic game-day situation.

#64: Staggered Tight Bags

Objective: To improve the defensive lineman's ability to develop the coordination with the same arm/same foot principle to make the pass rush more effective and increase the speed and quickness of the hands and feet

Equipment Needed: Vertical standing (weighted bottoms) bags or kickboxing training bags (bags that will not mover or tip over), quarterback bag (with arms), ball on a stick

Description: Place three bags in a single-file line one yard apart from each other and half yards staggered on a yard-line marker. The bags can be placed on the thick border sideline marker that accompanies a turf field. A fourth bag is place to the right or left of the last bag in line approximately five yards deep and five yards to the inside. Defensive linemen will form a line behind the first bag, which is opposite the last bag, simulating the quarterback. Each defensive lineman will align in a three-point outside shade stance (opposite shade of quarterback bag) on a yard-line marker, maintaining a neutral zone. The defensive lineman, on the snap, gets off the ball quickly and executes a pass rush technique (big rip, club flip, chop hoop). A pass rush stance and elongated first step is used to close the gap to the first bag. The same arm/same foot principle must be used to make the pass rush more effective. Once the move is complete, the defensive lineman approaches the next bag quickly and remains in a two-point stance for the rest of the drill. Once the last bag is complete, the defensive lineman points his toe toward the quarterback (bag or coach with ball in hand), rip escapes, and bursts to the bag to perform a proper strip-the-ball technique. Each pass rush technique should be performed to the right and left.

Coaching Point: The coach must encourage speed and quickness in executing each technique in the drill. This will make the defender more proficient in pass rush.

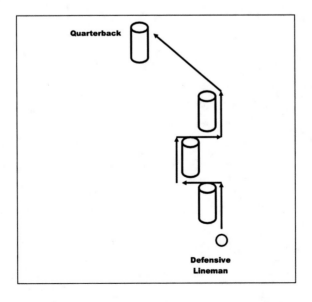

#65: Double Trouble Bags

Objective: To develop the ability of the defensive lineman to use a combination of hand parries and pass rush techniques to make the pass rush more effective

Equipment Needed: Vertical standing (weighted bottoms) bags or kickboxing training bags (bags that will not mover or tip over), quarterback bag (with arms), ball on a stick

Description: Place four bags as the corners in a seven-yard square. The two bags at the line of scrimmage will simulate the offensive blockers. The two bags in the back will be considered the quarterbacks. Place the line of scrimmage bags on a yard-line maker and establish a neutral zone. Defensive linemen align one on each line of scrimmage bag in a three-point outside edge stance. Each lineman will perform the drill independently,

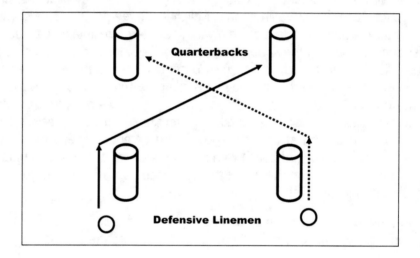

94

at a time. On the snap of the ball, one defensive lineman will perform the combination pass rush technique, escape, and burst the quarterback, which will be the bag opposite on the diagonal. The defensive lineman finishes the drill with a proper upright strip of the ball from the quarterback's upfield shoulder and hand. Once complete, the defensive lineman returns to the opposite line, and the next defensive lineman waits for the snap. Each pass rush technique should be performed to the right and left.

- Chop club flip: Initially, the defensive lineman will use an inside arm chop movement. This "ice pick and arm dent" on the blocker's arm near the wrist is followed by the club flip maneuver. The defensive lineman will be using his outside hand and foot technique, swat violently with an open hand, and simultaneously open (flip the hips) to clear the bag (blocker). The defender will point his toe to the inside, rip escape, and burst to the quarterback.

- Rip repunch: Initially, the defensive lineman will use an inside arm big rip maneuver. After the defender has thrown the rip and works upfield, the defensive lineman will back out of the rip move by pulling the rip out just as violently as the original throw. As the defender pulls the rip out, he will punch violently over the arm of the offensive blocker, step toward the quarterback, and swat at the ball. This repunch is a good pass rush maneuver when the defenders arm gets stuck under the blocker's arms and against his hips.

Coaching Point: A variation of this drill is to use live offensive blockers that provide a light resistance to the pass rusher.

#66: Square Bags

Objective: To improve the defensive lineman's ability to open his hips to violently club and clear the offensive blocker when using the club flip, jab olé, and turkey club pass rush techniques

Equipment Needed: Vertical standing (weighted bottoms) bags or kickboxing training bags (bags that will not mover or tip over), ball on a stick

Description: Place four bags on yard-line marker five yards apart in a square configuration. Defensive linemen will form a line behind the first bag. Each defensive lineman will align in a three-point outside shade stance, maintaining a neutral zone to commence the drill. On the snap, defensive lineman will get off the ball quickly and execute the pass rush club flip technique. The club will be performed violently with the outside arms, open hand, while flipping the hips to create power to clear the bag (blocker). The defender will rip escape burst to the next bag. The defensive line will remain an upright position, in a two-point stance, for the rest of the drill. The defender will repeat the same technique on the remainder of the bags, and once the last bag is complete, the defensive lineman will sprint through the bag in which he started the drill. Each pass rush technique should be performed to the right and left.

Coaching Points:

- The defensive lineman should be encouraged to sink his hips as he approaches each dummy, flip his hips before the violent club, and have his outside foot planted and drive off of it as he finishes the club.
- A variation of this drill is to use live offensive blockers that provide a light resistance to the pass rusher.

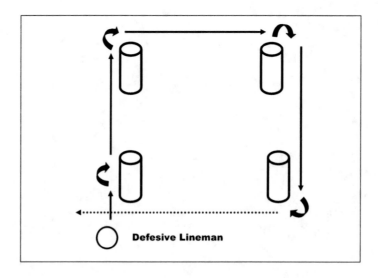

Defesive Lineman

#67: Upright Strip

Objective: To improve the ability of a pass rushing defensive lineman to stay on his feet as the quarterback states his throwing motion, and to develop the ability to high strip the ball and secure the quarterback in the event of escape

Equipment Needed: Vertical standing (weighted bottoms) bag, quarterback bag with arms or coach with ball in hand, cone, ball on a stick

Description: Place one bag on a yard-line marker with the quarterback bag with arms seven yards deep and seven yards to the inside of the pass rusher. A defensive lineman is aligned in his normal three-point pass rush stance on the edge of the line of scrimmage vertical standing dummy. On ball movement, the defensive lineman will use a speed rush toward the quarterback bag. The defensive linemen should rush the quarterback at three-quarter speed until he masters the technique. When the quarterback puts the ball in his cocked throwing position, the defensive lineman should grab cloth with his front hand and attempt a strip with his back hand. The drill should be performed from the right and left.

Coaching Points:

- The defensive lineman's focal point should be on the football in the quarterback's hands.
- Whenever the defender collapses on the quarterback, he should try to get to the quarterback's upfield shoulder.

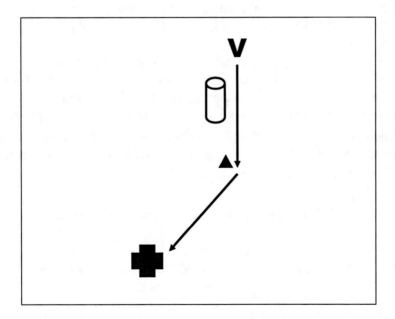

#68: Single-Hand Parries

Objective: To improve the ability of a pass rushing defensive lineman to use his hands to divert the offensive lineman's punches in another direction

Equipment Needed: None

Description: Pair off two defensive linemen. One defensive lineman will be the offensive lineman. Both linemen will be in a two-point stance. On the coach's command to commence the drill, the offensive blocker will shoot his hands toward the facing defensive lineman. The defensive lineman will either use the same or a combination of single-hand parries to keep the offensive lineman's hands of his body. After one parry is completed, each player will quickly reset and repeat the process. This drill should continue for a designed time period (20 to 30 seconds) or the number of thrusts by each player. Players will alternate between offensive and defensive personnel. The drill should be performed with the right- and left-handed parries. The single parries are as follows:

- Under tight: The defensive lineman takes inside hand, moves it under the wrist, and hooks over the offensive lineman's outside wrist.
- Over tight: The defensive lineman takes inside hand, moves it over the wrist, and hooks under the offensive lineman's outside wrist.
- Wrist grab: The defensive lineman takes outside hand and grabs the offensive lineman's wrist down and away while the inside arm is punching (the bicep) over the top.

Coaching Points:

- The defensive lineman's focal point should be on the offensive lineman's hands, and the hand movement should be rapid and violent by both players. This is a high-tempo drill.
- The coach should stress that if the blocker gets his hands locked onto the pass rusher, the result is usually a successful block and no pass rush. The pass rusher must protect his body with his hands as the offensive lineman hand punches the pass rusher in the chest to slow him down and maintain separation.
- A variation of the drill is that the defensive line after the parry can rip through the gap. If this is performed, the offensive lineman will flip to the other side and reshoot his hands.

#69: Transition Hand Parries

Objective: To enhance the ability of a defensive lineman when in a rundown situation to transition to a pass rush when the offensive blocker shows play-action or a quick set dropback protection using single or double sweeps

Equipment Needed: Ball on a stick

Description: Pair off two defensive linemen. One defensive lineman will be the offensive lineman. Both linemen will be in a three-point stance. On ball movement, the offensive blocker will get off as if it is a play-action pass or a quick pass set. The offensive lineman will shoot his hands. The defensive lineman will get off and engage the blocker with a two-hand jam. As the defender reads the pass set, the defensive lineman transitions to a pass rush parry. The parries that can be used are as follows:

- Single sweep: The defensive lineman will slide his hands back off from the two-handed jam to elbow (keep arms deep) and use an outside arm and hand to chop offensive lineman's arm down and away (single sweep) while bringing the inside arm over the top to punch the bicep area of the blocker. The defensive lineman's outside arm pins the offensive lineman's hip while the defender finishes with inside foot crossing over the offensive lineman's body, staying tight, moving the inside foot upfield, and ripping under the blocker's shoulder. The inside foot must get to the back of blocker's hip, and the footwork must be coordinated with arm/wrist movement.

- Double sweep (window wash): The defensive lineman will slide his hands back off from the two-handed jam to elbow (keep arms deep) and use both arms to chop offensive lineman's arm down and away (window wash). The defender finishes with inside foot crossing over the offensive lineman's body, staying tight, moving the inside foot upfield and ripping under the blocker's shoulder. The inside foot must get to the back of blocker's hip, and the footwork must be coordinated with arm/wrist movement.

- Double up: On engagement, the defensive lineman slides hands back off from the two-handed jam to elbow (keeping the arms deep), grab both wrists of the offensive lineman, and pop both wrists up to move the blocker's wrists and arms up. The defender finishes with the inside foot crossing over the offensive lineman's body, staying tight, moving inside foot upfield, and ripping under the blocker's shoulder. The inside foot must get to the back of blocker's hip, and the footwork must be coordinated with arm/wrist movement.

Coaching Points:

- All drills should be performed with the right- and left-handed parries.
- The coach must emphasize to the defensive lineman that the most crucial technique is that the pass rusher's hands and feet are tied together, working as one when the move is in progress.
- The defensive lineman's focal point should be on the offensive lineman's hands, and the hand movement should be rapid and violent by both players. This is a high-tempo drill.
- The coach should stress that if the blocker gets his hands locked onto the pass rusher, the result is usually a successful block and no pass rush. The pass rusher must protect his body with his hands as the offensive lineman hand punches the pass rusher in the chest to slow him down and maintain separation.

9

Pass Rush Moves: Block Protection Development vs. the Pass

#70: Vertical Set Read and React

Objective: To enhance the ability of a defensive lineman who is aligned on the edge to read and react when attacking a vertical set pass protection

Equipment Needed: Ball on a stick

Description: Pair off two players. One player will be the offensive lineman. The defensive linemen will be in a three-point outside shaded stance while the offensive lineman can be in a two- or three-point stance. Align the players on a yard-line marker, and establish a neutral zone. On ball movement, the offensive blocker will get off quickly, performing a vertical set pass protection. In vertical set pass protection, the offensive line will retreat in a backpedal-style fashion, similar to the technique of a defensive back. The goal by the offensive lineman is to lose as much ground, while staying square before making contact with the defender. The offensive lineman will shoot his hands when the defensive lineman is within range. The defensive lineman will get off quickly vertically, read the vertical set pass protection as he closes rapidly, and then react to the type of vertical set. The read and reaction must occur with four yards (the point of attack) of the line of scrimmage. Once the move is made, the defensive lineman must escape, finish, and burst to the quarterback. The drill should be performed from the right and left edges. The three reads and pass rush moves that are associated with those actions are as follows:

- Soft strike: When the offensive lineman vertical sets and turns his shoulder toward the pass rusher and puts both hands on the defensive lineman, the defender must get to the blocker as quickly as he can and use a power move (bull rush, bull rush with a push-pull, bull rush with slingshot).
- Firm deflect: When the offensive lineman keeps his shoulders parallel to the line of scrimmage, kick slides straight back, and uses one hand on the defensive lineman (true vertical set), the defender must use a speed rush move (dip-and-rip), big rip, club flip, chop club flip, chop hoop, double sweep (window wash), or rip repunch that destroys the blocker's jam.

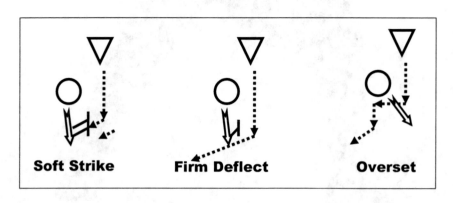

Soft Strike   **Firm Deflect**   **Overset**

- Overset: When the offensive lineman kick slides off the vertical plane and blocks the straight line lane of the defensive lineman's rush, the defender must use a counter move (race and counter club, fake chop wheel).

Coaching Points:

- The coach must emphasize to the defensive lineman that the vertical set pass protection causes a lack of leverage by the defensive linemen once they reach the point of attack. A defensive lineman, in his crouched stance, must stay low and explode the line of scrimmage on pass protection. The problem that occurs when their target (offensive lineman) retreats, the tendency is for the defensive line to run more upright, thereby losing all of their leverage and their "power" they had when coming off the line of scrimmage. So, in effect, the offense has taken the explosiveness out of the defensive line by moving their target farther away from them. What is critical is that the pass rusher's hands and feet are tied together, working as one when the move is in progress.
- The defensive lineman pass rush creed should be "Going to a fire/I'm on fire." Whenever you see a fire truck, there will be little kids chasing the fire truck. The pass rusher needs to demonstrate that same sense of urgency, like they are on the way to a fire. In addition, whenever you watch a movie that has a stuntman who is on fire, he is running around like crazy. Pass rushers must perform like they are on fire.
- The defensive lineman's focal point should be on the offensive lineman's hands and the hand movement should be rapid and violent by both players.

#71: Power Move—Bull Rush

Objective: To teach the defensive lineman the bull rush technique

Equipment Needed: Blocking board or low agility bag, ball on a stick

Description: The ball is used as a movement key for the defensive lineman's takeoff. The offensive blocker stands at one end of the board or agility bag with his feet straddling the board (bag). The blocker takes a good two-point stance pass protection stance. The defensive lineman assumes a position facing the offensive blocker. When the coach moves the ball, the defensive lineman takes off. The defensive lineman throws his hands on the snap and engages the blocker with two hands. The defender should sink his hips, keep his head back, and his back flat so that he maintains leverage on the blocker. The defensive lineman should churn his feet and drive the blocker backward until he pushes the blocker the length of the board.

Coaching Points:

- The coach should emphasize that the defensive lineman punch violently on the breastplate with both hands. The hands must get inside the blocker's hands and make contact on top of the blockers numbers.

- The blow is struck with the palms and heels of the hands and must delivered with enough power to force the offensive man backward or at the minimum, shift the blocker's weight from the balls of his feet to his heels. This limits the blocker's ability to react quickly to changes of direction by the rusher.
- As the hands strike the blow, the defensive lineman must grab cloth on the offensive lineman's jersey and the elbows should lock, thereby bringing into use additional force of the back muscles.
- The defensive lineman's helmet must be lower than the blocker's chin by the pass rusher having good bend (or flexion) in the ankles, knees, and hips. This helps to maintain leverage on the blocker.
- The pass rusher should use short, choppy quick steps while executing the power rush technique. The defensive lineman must avoid long strides, which compromises the defender's power base.
- This power pass rush technique is most effectively used by inside rushers versus the three- and five-step dropback pass types as well as play-action on rundowns.

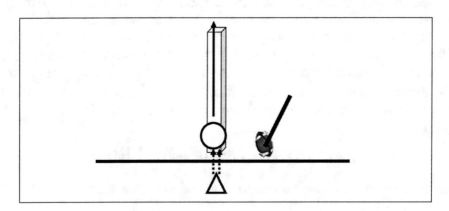

#72: Push-Pull Move

Objective: To develop the defensive lineman's ability to perform a push-pull move when using the bull rush technique

Equipment Needed: None

Description: Two players stand facing each other an arm's distance apart. One player role plays the part of an offensive lineman performing as dropback pass protection while the other player is the defensive pass rusher. The offensive lineman assumes a two-point pass protection ready stance with his head back and his knees bent. The blocker places his hands on the numbers of the defensive lineman. The defensive lineman will assume the correct posture for initiating a hands-on, pass rushing power move (bull rush). On the coach's command, the defender will slide one of his hands to the triceps of the blocker while the other is grabbing cloth (the hand can widen slightly). Using both arms, running the feet, and keeping a low pad level, the defensive lineman drives the blocker backward so the blocker's weight shifts to his heels. The defender immediately follows with push move on the arm where the defender is grabbing the triceps and using a pull move with the other arm jerking the blocker's shoulders forward. The defensive lineman then finishes the move by releasing the far arm and ripping underneath the opposite armpit of the blocker. The rip is made in the manner of a violent uppercut punch. As the punch is made across the blocker's body, the foot corresponding to the side of the punching hand quickly swings across the defensive lineman's body and plants in a near heel-to-toe relationship outside the blocker's foot. The defensive lineman clears the blocker and continues to rush toward the passing quarterback. The drill continues for several repetitions to each side, and the players exchange roles.

Coaching Points:

- The coach should emphasize that the defensive lineman punch violently on the breastplate with both hands. The hands must get inside the blocker's hands and make contact on top of the blocker's numbers.
- The blow is struck with the palms and heels of the hands and must be delivered with enough power to force the offensive man backward or, at the minimum, shift the blocker's weight from the balls of his feet to his heels. This limits the blocker's ability to react quickly to changes of direction by the rusher.
- As the hands strike the blow, the defensive lineman must grab cloth on the offensive lineman's jersey, and the elbows should lock, thereby bringing into use additional force of the back muscles.
- The defensive lineman's helmet must be lower than the blocker's chin by the pass rusher having good bend (or flexion) in the ankles, knees, and hips. This helps to maintain leverage on the blocker.
- The pass rusher should use short, choppy quick steps while executing the power rush technique. The defensive lineman must avoid long strides which compromises the defender's power base.
- This bull rush pass rushing technique is most effectively used by inside rushers versus the three- and five-step dropback pass types as well as play-action on rundowns.

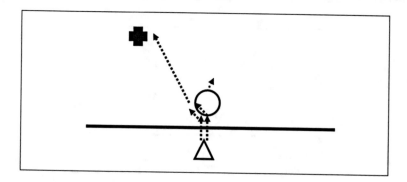

#73: Rip Move

Objective: To develop the ability of the defensive lineman to perform the rip move

Equipment Needed: None

Description: Two players stand facing each other an arm's distance apart. One player role plays the part of an offensive lineman performing as dropback pass protection while the other player is the defensive pass rusher. The offensive lineman assumes a two-point pass protection ready stance with his head back and his knees bent. The blocker places his hands on the front of the jersey of the defensive lineman. The defensive lineman will assume the correct posture for initiating a hands-on pass rushing move such as a power bull rush or push pull technique. On the coach's command, the defender will slide one of his hands to the triceps of the blocker while the other is grabbing cloth (the hand can widen slightly). Using both arms, running the feet, and keeping a low pad level, the defensive lineman drives the blocker backward so the blocker's weight shifts to his heels. As the defensive lineman feels the offensive lineman's weight shifting backward, he releases the arm and rips with his off-hand underneath the opposite armpit of the blocker. A rush from the left side begins his rip move with his right hand, while the rusher from the right side uses his left hand. The rip should be made in the manner of a violent uppercut. As the punch is made across the blocker's body, the foot corresponding to the side of the punching hand quickly swings across the defensive lineman's body and plants in a near heel-to-toe relationship outside the blocker's foot. The defensive lineman freezes in that position and checks the positioning of his swing foot in relationship to the blocker's foot. When the rip is completed, the defensive lineman should have gained an upfield advantage of the blocker. The drill continues for several repetitions to each side and the players exchange roles.

Coaching Points:

- The defender should keep his thumbs up when he grabs the back of the blocker's upper arm.
- The defender should push the blocker's shoulder backward with his up hand as he uses his off hand to rip across the blocker's body.

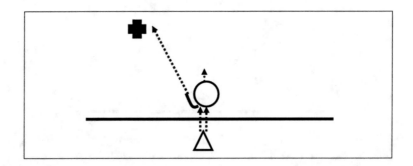

#74: Slingshot Move

Objective: To develop the defensive lineman's ability to perform a pull down slingshot move when using the bull rush technique

Equipment Needed: None

Description: Two players stand facing each other an arm's distance apart. One player role plays the part of an offensive lineman performing as dropback pass protection while the other player is the defensive pass rusher. The offensive lineman assumes a two-point pass protection ready stance with his head back and his knees bent. The blocker places his hands on the numbers of the defensive lineman. The defensive lineman will assume the correct posture for initiating a hands-on, pass rushing power move (bull rush). On the coach's command, the defender will slide one of his hands to the triceps of the blocker while the other is grabbing cloth (hand can widen slightly). Using both arms, running the feet, and keeping a low pad level, the defensive lineman drives the blocker backward so the blocker's weight shifts to his heels. As the defensive lineman feels the offensive lineman's weight shifting backward, the defensive lineman uses his weight and arms to propel the blocker forward and down. This throw (pull down/shrug) should finish with a rip move. The defensive lineman makes the rip with a violent uppercut punch opposite the side of the throw. As the punch is made across the blocker's body, the foot corresponding to the side of the punching hand quickly swings across the defensive lineman's body and plants in a near heel-to-toe relationship outside the blocker's foot. The defensive lineman clears the blocker and continues to rush toward the passing quarterback. The drill continues for several repetitions to each side, and the players exchange roles.

Coaching Points:

- The coach should emphasize that the defensive lineman punch violently on the breastplate with both hands. The hands must get inside the blocker's hands and make contact on top of the blockers numbers.
- The blow is struck with the palms and heels of the hands and must be delivered with enough power to force the offensive man backward or, at the minimum, shift the blocker's weight from the balls of his feet to his heels. This limits the blocker's ability to react quickly to changes of direction by the rusher.

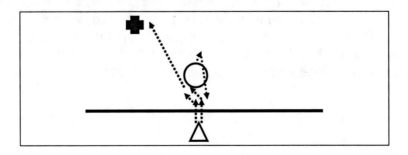

- As the hands strike the blow, the defensive lineman must grab cloth on the offensive lineman's jersey, and the elbows should lock, thereby bringing into use additional force of the back muscles.
- The defensive lineman's helmet must be lower than the blocker's chin by the pass rusher having good bend (or flexion) in the ankles, knees, and hips. This helps to maintain leverage on the blocker.
- The pass rusher should use short, choppy quick steps while executing the power rush technique. The defensive lineman must avoid long strides, which compromises the defender's power base.
- This bull rush pass rushing technique is most effectively used by inside rushers versus the three- and five-step dropback pass types as well as play-action on rundowns.

#75: Chop Rip Move—Edge Rush

Objective: To teach a defensive lineman, mostly defensive ends, an edge speed rush that incorporates a chop rip technique

Equipment Needed: A free-standing form tackling dummy with or without arms, ball on a stick

Description: Aligning on the edge of an offensive blocker with a pass rush stance, the defensive lineman takes off on the movement of the ball. The offensive lineman vertical sets quickly. The defensive lineman explodes out of his stance, stepping forward with the ballside leg, and races straight up the field. The defensive lineman will read the set of the offensive lineman and react with a planned move. This chop rip pass rush move will be used when the offensive tackle kick slides straight back (firm deflect) and sets inside the defender. On the third step (within four yards), the defensive lineman plants the ballside foot, lowers his body while chopping down violently on the extended arm of the offensive blocker, and driving the same arm back up aggressively through the hip and shoulders of the offensive lineman. The plant foot should have the toe pointed toward the quarterback, and the outside arm should be thrown around the blockers. This helps maintaining leverage by the defender on the blocker. The fourth step will be with the outside foot, and it should be planted to square the defensive lineman's hips toward the quarterback. Once clearing the blocker, the pass rusher should accelerate to the quarterback and perform a sack. A free-standing dummy should be positioned at the quarterback position. To simulate the quarterback sack, the defensive lineman should club the dummy with his inside arm. His outside arm should be kept free unless the dummy has arms, then the rusher can attempt to strip the football. In a game situation, the defensive lineman should use his outside arm to rake the quarterback's throwing arm. The drill continues for several repetitions to the right and left sides for each defender.

- If the move has not been successful within four yards, the pass rusher must convert to a bull rush.
- A variation to the chop would be to use a wrist grab with one or both hands and then dip-and-rip around the offensive blocker's hip.
- The coach must emphasize that the player who is the offensive lineman must keeps his shoulders parallel to the line of scrimmage, kick slide straight back quickly, and use one hand on the defensive lineman (true vertical set).
- To simulate a moving quarterback, the coach may substitute a player at the quarterback position. In this case, the defensive lineman should only tag the quarterback above the waist with two hands.
- The coach needs to inform the pass rusher if he is coming from the quarterback's dominant side (the side quarterback is looking to throw), the throwing arm of the quarterback is the pass rusher's aiming point for the pressure and contain. If the rusher is coming from the non-dominant side, the rusher should aim for the shoulder of the quarterback's non-throwing arm.

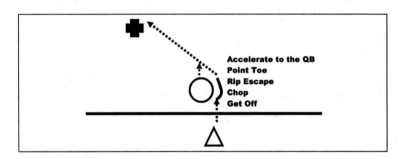

#76: Chop Club Flip Move

Objective: To teach a defensive lineman, mostly defensive ends, an edge speed rush that incorporates a chop club flip the hips technique

Equipment Needed: A free-standing form tackling dummy with or without arms, ball on a stick

Description: Aligning on the edge of an offensive blocker with a pass rush stance, the defensive lineman takes off on the movement of the ball. The offensive lineman vertical sets quickly. The defensive lineman explodes out of his stance, stepping forward with the ballside leg, and races straight up the field. The defensive lineman will read the set of the offensive lineman and react with a planned move. This chop club flip pass rush move will be used when the offensive tackle kick slides straight back (firm deflect) and sets inside the defender. On the third step, the defensive lineman plants the ballside foot, lowers his body while chopping down violently on the extended arm of the offensive blocker. This "ice pick and arm dent" on the blocker's near arm wrist is followed by the club flip maneuver. The defensive lineman will be using his outside hand and foot technique, swat violently with an open hand, and simultaneously open (flip the hips) to clear the bag (blocker). The defender will point his toe to the inside, rip escape, and burst to the quarterback. This helps maintaining leverage by the defender on the blocker. Once clearing the blocker, the pass rusher should accelerate to quarterback and perform a sack. A free standing dummy should be positioned at the quarterback position. To simulate the quarterback sack, the defensive lineman should club the dummy with his inside arm. His outside arm should be kept free unless the dummy has arms, then the rusher can attempt to strip the football. In a game situation, the defensive lineman should use his outside arm to rake the quarterback's throwing arm. The drill continues for several repetitions to the right and left sides for each defender.

Coaching Point:

- The coach must emphasize that the defensive lineman should sprint to get even with the pass blocker before he clubs and flips the hips ("If you're even, you're leavin'.").
- The pass rusher can use two techniques to move their feet to enhance the opening of the hips when clubbing the offensive lineman.
  - ✓ The defensive lineman can quickly lateral shuffle to reduce the surface area for the blocker to rejam.
  - ✓ Instead of clubbing the defensive lineman can wrap his outside arm around the blocker's back and grab cloth and carioca the feet to clear the offensive lineman.
- If the move has not been successful within four yards, the pass rusher must convert to a bull rush.
- The coach must emphasize that the player who is the offensive lineman must keep his shoulders parallel to the line of scrimmage, kick slide straight back quickly, and use one hand on the defensive lineman (true vertical set).
- The coach needs to inform the pass rusher if he is coming from the quarterback's dominant side (the side quarterback is looking to throw), the throwing arm of the quarterback is the pass rusher's aiming point for the pressure and contain. If the rusher is coming from the non-dominant side, the rusher should aim for the shoulder of the quarterback's non-throwing arm.

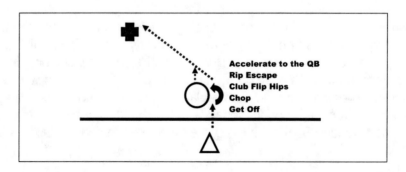

#77: Window Wash Move

Objective: To teach a defensive lineman, mostly defensive ends, an edge speed rush that incorporates double-arm sweep

Equipment Needed: A free-standing form tackling dummy with or without arms, ball on a stick

Description: Aligning on the edge of an offensive blocker with a pass rush stance, the defensive lineman takes off on the movement of the ball. The offensive lineman vertical sets quickly. The defensive lineman explodes out of his stance, stepping forward with the ballside leg, and races straight up the field. The defensive lineman will read the set of the offensive lineman and react with a planned move. This window-wash maneuver pass will be used when the offensive tackle kick slides straight back (firm deflect) and sets inside the defender. When the blocker extends his arm to the defender's chest, the defensive lineman uses both arms in circular motion (window wash) toward the ball to knock down the jam of the offensive lineman. The defender will continue with planting the ballside foot on third or fifth step, pointing the toes and squaring his hips toward the quarterback. The defender will dip-and-rip and accelerate to the quarterback to perform a sack. This helps maintaining leverage by the defender on the blocker. A free-standing dummy should be positioned at the quarterback position. To simulate the quarterback sack, the defensive lineman should club the dummy with his inside arm. His outside arm should be kept free unless the dummy has arms, then the rusher can attempt to strip the football. In a game situation, the defensive lineman should use his outside arm to rake the quarterback's throwing arm. The drill continues for several repetitions to the right and left sides for each defender.

Coaching Points:

- The defender should always keep his hands above his waist so there are no wasted movements.
- The coach must emphasize that the defensive lineman should sprint to get even with the pass blocker before he uses the double sweep move.

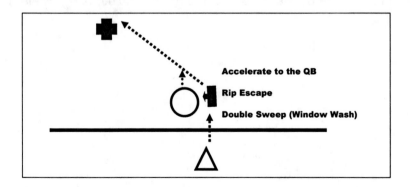

- If the move has not been successful within four yards, the pass rusher must convert to a bull rush.
- The coach must emphasize that the player who is the offensive lineman must keep his shoulders parallel to the line of scrimmage, kick slide straight back quickly, and use one hand on the defensive lineman (true vertical set).
- The coach needs to inform the pass rusher if he is coming from the quarterback's dominant side (side the quarterback is looking to throw), the throwing arm of the quarterback is the pass rusher's aiming point for the pressure and contain. If the rusher is coming from the non-dominant side the rusher should aim for the shoulder of the quarterback's non-throwing arm.

#78: Rip Repunch Move

Objective: To teach a defensive lineman that if the arm gets stuck on a big rip move to pull out of rip (rip counter) and use a punch (over tight) followed by opening (flipping) the hips

Equipment Needed: A free-standing form tackling dummy with or without arms, ball on a stick

Description: Aligning on the edge of an offensive blocker with a pass rush stance, the defensive lineman takes off on the movement of the ball. The offensive lineman vertical sets quickly. The defensive lineman explodes out of his stance, stepping forward with the ballside leg, and races straight up the field. The defensive lineman will read the set of the offensive lineman and react with a planned move. This rip counter maneuver will be used when the offensive tackle kick slides straight back (firm deflect) and sets inside the defender. Initially, the defensive lineman will use an inside arm big rip maneuver. After the defender has thrown the rip as he works up field, the defensive lineman will back out of the rip move by pulling the rip out just as violently as the original throw. As the defender pulls the rip out, he will punch violently over the arm of the offensive blocker. The defensive lineman will punch the bicep of the blocker. As the punch occurs, the defensive lineman will flip his hips and reach with the outside arm to grab the back of offensive lineman's shoulder and pull him away from the quarterback, while simultaneously using the ballside hand to grab cloth and pull the blocker forward and dipping and rip underneath the offensive lineman's shoulder. The defender will accelerate to the quarterback to perform a sack. This helps maintaining leverage by the defender on the blocker. A free-standing dummy should be positioned at the quarterback position. To simulate the quarterback sack, the defensive lineman should club the dummy with his inside arm. His outside arm should be kept free unless the dummy has arms, then the rusher can attempt to strip the football. In a game situation, the defensive lineman should use his outside arm to rake the quarterback's throwing arm. The drill continues for several repetitions to the right and left sides for each defender.

Coaching Points:

- This repunch is a good pass rush maneuver when the defender's arm gets stuck under the blocker's arms and against his hips.
- The defensive lineman must get his hips past the blocker, point the toe to the passer, and accelerate (burst) toward quarterback.
- If the move has not been successful within four yards, the pass rusher must convert to a bull rush.
- The coach must emphasize that the player who is the offensive lineman must keep his shoulders parallel to the line of scrimmage, kick slide straight back quickly, and use one hand on the defensive lineman (true vertical set).

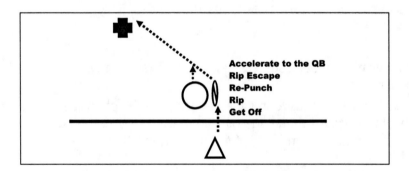

#79: Race and Counter Move

Objective: To improve the ability of a pass rushing defensive lineman, mostly the defensive end, to counter an overset by an offensive lineman

Equipment Needed: A free-standing form tackling dummy with or without arms, ball on a stick

Description: Aligning on the edge of an offensive blocker with a pass rush stance, the defensive lineman takes off on the movement of the ball. The offensive lineman will overset. The defensive lineman explodes out of his stance, stepping forward with the ballside leg, and races straight up the field. The defensive lineman will read the set of the offensive lineman and react with a planned move. When the offensive lineman kick slides off the vertical plane and blocks the straight line lane of the defensive lineman's rush, the defender must use one of the counter moves (race and counter club or fake counter wheel). As the defensive lineman gets off upfield from a wide edge alignment, he reads that the offensive lineman has overset and blocked his vertical path. On the fourth step, the defender will plant his outside foot, keep his shoulders square to line of scrimmage as he shuffles across the blocker's body. Once the defender makes his lateral movement, he clubs with inside arm, rips with outside arm, while dipping his shoulder under the inside shoulder pad of the blocker. The defensive lineman will sprint vertically upfield to keep leverage on the passer and then point the toe, accelerate to the ball, and rush the back shoulder of the quarterback. The drill continues for several repetitions to the right and left sides for each defender.

Coaching Points:

- If the move has not been successful within four yards, the pass rusher must convert to a bull rush.
- The coach must emphasize that the player who is the offensive lineman must keep his shoulders parallel to the line of scrimmage, kick slide quickly on a sharp angle to the outside to block the lane of the pass rusher.

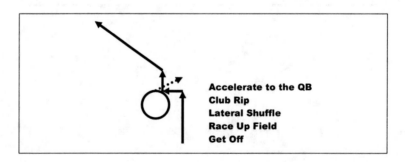

#80: Fake Chop Wheel Move

Objective: To improve the ability of a pass rushing defensive lineman, mostly defensive end, to counter an overset by an offensive lineman with an outside hand chop, spin and club maneuver

Equipment Needed: A free-standing form tackling dummy with or without arms, ball on a stick

Description: Aligning on the edge of an offensive blocker with a pass rush stance, the defensive lineman takes off on the movement of the ball. The offensive lineman will overset. The defensive lineman explodes out of his stance, stepping forward with the ballside leg, and races straight up the field. The defensive lineman will read the set of the offensive lineman and react with a planned move. As the defensive lineman gets off upfield from a wide edge alignment, he reads that the offensive lineman has overset and has blocked his vertical path. On the fourth step, the pass rush sinks his hips, chops with his outside hand, plants his outside foot, and drives off of it. This chop attempts to place the arms and body of the blocker off-balance. The defensive lineman aggressively swings his inside arm around the blocker's hip closest to the quarterback. As the club is in progress, the defender keeps his feet moving, performing the spin in the opposite direction (wheel). Once the defender completes his club and spin, he maintains a low pad level sprint vertically upfield to keep leverage on the passer, and then points the toes, accelerates to the ball, and rushes the back shoulder of the quarterback. The drill continues for several repetitions to the right and left sides for each defender.

Coaching Points:

- The defensive lineman must keep his should pad level lower that the blocker's through out the entire move and held tight to the blocker.
- If the move has not been successful within four yards, the pass rusher must convert to a bull rush.
- The coach must emphasize that the player who is the offensive lineman must keep his shoulders parallel to the line of scrimmage, kick slide quickly on a sharp angle to the outside to block the lane of the pass rusher.

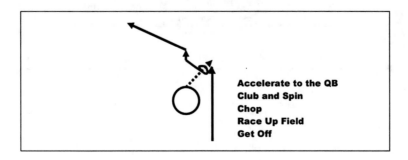

Accelerate to the QB
Club and Spin
Chop
Race Up Field
Get Off

#81: Rip and Pick Move

Objective: To develop an interior pass rushing defensive lineman, mostly tackles and noses, and to rip and grab the offensive lineman's arm to gain a leverage advantage

Equipment Needed: A free-standing form tackling dummy with or without arms, ball on a stick

Description: Playing over an offensive blocker, the defensive interior lineman takes off on ball movement. The defensive lineman stance will use an outside shade stance with the inside foot back. Aligning on the edge of an offensive blocker with a pass rush stance, the defensive lineman takes off on the movement of the ball. The offensive lineman will short vertical set. The defensive line, on this third or fifth step (depends on the depth of the offensive lineman's set) will big rip with inside arm and lean into the blocker's hip (keep hips tight to blocker). As the rip is in progress, the fourth or sixth step, the defensive lineman will use his outside hand and arm to grab and lift (pick) the offensive blocker's outside arm. The defender points the inside toes to the quarterback, dips under the blocker's pad level, and races to the passer. The drill continues for several repetitions to the right and left sides for each defender.

Coaching Point:

- The defensive lineman must continue to lift the rip, pinning the offensive lineman's movement to gain a leverage advantage while not widening the pass rush.
- The defensive lineman must keep his should pad level lower that the blocker's throughout the entire move and hold tight to the blocker.
- If the move has not been successful within four yards, the pass rusher must convert to a bull rush.

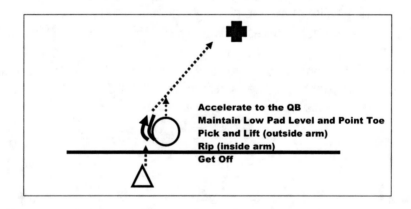

Accelerate to the QB
Maintain Low Pad Level and Point Toe
Pick and Lift (outside arm)
Rip (inside arm)
Get Off

#82: Stab-and-Grab Move

Objective: To develop an interior pass rushing defensive lineman, mostly tackles and noses, who can jam the blocker with the inside hand and grab his outside arm to gain a leverage advantage on a pass protecting offensive lineman

Equipment Needed: A free-standing form tackling dummy with or without arms, ball on a stick

Description: Playing over an offensive blocker, the defensive interior lineman takes off on ball movement. The defensive lineman stance will use an outside shade stance with the inside foot back. Aligning on the edge of an offensive blocker with a pass rush stance, the defensive lineman takes off on the movement of the ball. The offensive lineman will short vertical set. The execution of this technique commences with the defensive line on this third or fifth step, stabbing hard with the inside arm (heart punch) to the near number of the offensive blocker. As the defender continues to run his feet, he uses his outside hand, grabs the outside arm of the blocker at the wrist (weakest point), and violently lifts the blocker's arm up. This maneuver should turn the offensive lineman's shoulders as the defender move upfield, opening the gate toward the quarterback. The drill continues for several repetitions to the right and left sides for each defender.

Coaching Points:

- If the defensive lineman misses the stab-and-grab move, he must immediately go to the power/bull rush to maintain the pass rush lane.
- The defensive lineman must keep his shoulder pad level lower that the blocker's throughout the entire move and hold tight to the blocker.

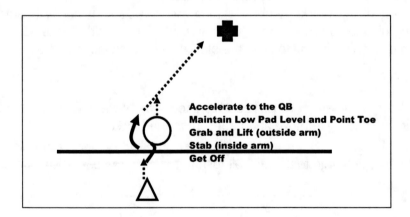

Accelerate to the QB
Maintain Low Pad Level and Point Toe
Grab and Lift (outside arm)
Stab (inside arm)
Get Off

#83: Foot Counter Move

Objective: To improve the ability of an interior pass rushing defensive lineman, mostly tackles and noses, to use footwork counter maneuvers to gain a leverage advantage on an offensive blocker

Equipment Needed: Ball on a stick

Description: A defensive lineman is positioned so that he is shaded on an offensive lineman. The drill begins by having the defensive lineman get off on ball movement while the offensive lineman is short vertical setting. Just prior to engaging the blocker, the defender will execute one of the two foot counter moves, depending on the stance that he uses. Once the defender clears the blocker, he accelerates to the passer while maintaining his pass rush lane. The drill continues for several repetitions to the right and left sides for each defender. The foot counters are as follows:

- Turkey club: The defensive lineman aligns with his back foot away from the ball. On ball movement, the defender will race upfield, and on the third step, the defensive lineman jab steps with his outside foot, planting it hard in the ground. The defensive lineman will shuffle lateral across chest of the blocker, club with his inside arm on the inside of the blocker while simultaneously flipping his hips. The defender will cross over with his feet and get the original outside foot outside the blocker's foot. Once the defensive lineman clears the blocker, he will use a rip escape and accelerate to the quarterback.
- Jab olé: The defensive lineman aligns with his normal edge rush stance with his foot closes to the ball back. On ball movement, the defender will take a slant step (45-degree angle) to inside shoulder of the blocker. The defender's next step will be straight up the field. This should have the offensive lineman shifting his weight to the inside with a power step. The defensive lineman now shuffles laterally across the chest of the blocker while clubbing the outside shoulder with outside arm, flipping his hips and getting his original inside foot outside the blocker's outside foot, dipping and ripping to clear the blocker and accelerating to the ball.

Coaching Points:

- The defensive lineman must keep his should pad level lower that the blocker's throughout the entire move and hold tight to the blocker.
- If the defensive lineman does not complete the turkey club or jab olé move, he must immediately go to power/bull rush to maintain the pass rush lane blocker.

10

Two- and Three-Man Games and Team Pass Rush: Block Protection Development vs. the Pass

#84: Two-Man Quick Games

Objective: To improve the techniques and timing of two-man stunts that involves two defensive linemen, where one is a slanter that attempts to grab an offensive lineman in order to free up the looper who is wrapping around the slanter with the games commencing on the snap of the ball

Equipment Needed: Ball on a stick

Description: The initial stages of practice on two-man games should be done with four defensive linemen. Two serve as offensive blockers, and the remaining two as pass rushers. The offensive blockers should use quick or short, vertical pass sets. The 2-on-2 games, for example, will involve defensive ends with interior defensive linemen (tackle, noses) or two interior linemen. When using interior defender games, a third offensive lineman should be added to assume the center position. Having the center lined up between the guards provides the exact spacing they will face when executing these games against an offensive team. The two defensive linemen are positioned in their proper alignments according to the defensive front and strength call. On the snap of the ball, the defensive linemen should perform the quick stunt called by the coach— one half of the stunt being done by the slanter, while the other half by the looper. Have players perform this drill with different two-man game combinations from the right and left sides. Do several repetitions of each.

Coaching Points:

- The defensive lineman who is the slanter or penetrator must slant into the predetermined key (offensive lineman) reading the key's blocking scheme (man/ zone protection). On the snap of the ball, the slanter will take a clear step, which is a six-inch, 45-degree directional step with the near foot directly to the far foot of the offensive lineman. The defensive lineman will drive off the far leg and explode toward the key reading the protection. If the defensive lineman reads that his key is working on the looper, he will slant to the back hip of that offensive blocker, push off his hip, and sprint vertically upfield. If the key closes toward the slanter, the slanter will grab the offensive lineman pulling him away from the looper. With both situations, the slanter must maintain low pad level, which will help maintain balance and leverage. If the blocker moves away with a reach block, the slanter will flatten out down the line and try to get to the outside shoulder of the blocker. The slanter must get his hands on the blocker to prevent him from running up onto the linebackers.

- The looper must sell the 1-on-1 rush. The looper is the defensive lineman who will twist around the slanter after selling the 1-on-1 rush. On ball movement, the looper will get off just like a normal pass rush vertical up the field. The looper will read on the run. If a reach block occurs, the looper will play the run with his normal push-pull reach technique. If the defender reads pass, he will continue to race upfield, selling the 1-on-1 pass rush until the slanter has penetrated the gap or displaced the blocker. Once the slanter's hat is in the crack, the looper steps flat (laterally) by planting his outside foot firmly and opening his leg and hip as if he was an offensive guard pulling. The looper then twists as tight to the slanter as possible, reading the offensive lineman he is moving toward. If the offensive blocker turns toward him with his far shoulder pointing upfield, looper will attack that shoulder to maintain his pass rush lane. If the blocker sits flat to the line of scrimmage, the looper will bull rush that offensive lineman. If the blocker turns away, like zone pass protection, the looper will push off his near hip and rush vertically upfield.

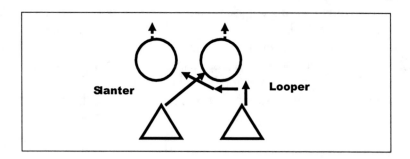

#85: Two-Man Delay Games

Objective: To improve the techniques and timing of two-man stunts that involves two defensive linemen twisting after the defensive linemen bull rush the offensive blockers

Equipment Needed: Ball on a stick

Description: The initial stages of practice on two-man games should be done with four defensive linemen. Two serve as offensive blockers, and the remaining two as pass rushers. The offensive blockers should utilize deep sets. The 2-on-2 games, for example, will involve defensive ends with interior defensive linemen (tackle, noses) or two interior linemen. The offensive blockers should use quick or short vertical pass sets. The two defensive linemen are positioned in their proper alignments, according to the defensive front and strength call. On the snap of the ball, the two defensive linemen will be the slanters, and the third defender will be the looper. If the defensive end is the looper, he will use a long stick technique. In a long stick, the defensive end will not rush upfield first then loop. He will be aligned six inches off the ball, take a lateral first step, and swing his ballside arm as if he was pulling. He will then take two more steps. The defensive end will plant on his third step and read the third offensive blocker away (center). Have players perform this drill with different three-man game combinations from the right and left sides. Do several repetitions of each.

Coaching Points:

- Both defensive linemen must get off the ball, bull rush the blockers driving them back. On the "go" command by the slanter (drive blocker back two steps), both defenders will execute the twist. The slanter must explode toward the adjacent blocker, aiming at his inside arm. The defender will read the hip of the blocker. If he turns away from him, the slanter will push off the hip of the blocker and rush upfield. If the blocker cuts off the upfield path, the slanter must play over the top of that blocker to maintain the pass rush lane and possibly contain.

- The looper must be patient until the slanter has sliced through into the backfield or pulled the offensive lineman away. The looper should come as tight as possible to the slanter, thus creating a pick situation. If the looper's key (slanter's original blocker) turns toward him with his far shoulder pointing upfield, the looper will attack that shoulder to maintain his pass rush lane. If the blocker sits flat to the line of scrimmage, the looper will bull rush that offensive lineman. If the blocker turns away, like zone pass protection, the looper will push off his near hip and rush vertically upfield. If an interior lineman is the looper, he will use the same technique as the looper in the two-man game.

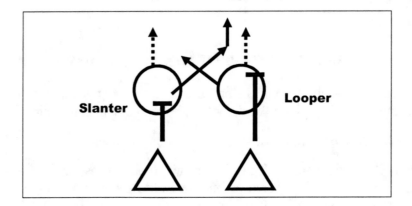

#86: Three-Man Quick Games

Objective: To teach a three-man quick stunt for attacking dropback pass and turnback protection

Equipment Needed: Ball on a stick

Description: In order to teach and practice three-man games, the offensive should consist of three players. This group of players will provide the proper personnel spacing to run any combination of the three-man games. The defensive personnel can include a defensive end with two interior linemen (tackle, nose) or three interior linemen. The offensive blockers should utilize deep sets. The 2-on-2 games, for example, will involve defensive ends with interior defensive linemen (tackle, noses) or two interior linemen. When using interior defender games, a third offensive lineman should be added to assume the center position. Having the center lined up between the guards provides the exact spacing they will face when executing these games against an offensive team. The two defensive linemen are positioned in their proper alignments, according to the defensive front and strength call. On the snap of the ball, the defensive linemen will bull rush and drive the offensive lineman back for two steps, and then perform the delay stunt called by the coach—one half of the stunt being done by the slanter, while the other half by the looper after the bull rushing first. Have players perform this drill with different three-man game combinations from the right and left sides. Do several repetitions of each.

Coaching Points:

- The defensive linemen who are the slanters must get off the ball quickly. The slanter must explode toward the adjacent blocker, aiming at his inside arm. The defender will read the hip of the blocker. If he turns away from him, the slanter will push off the hip of the blocker and rush upfield. If the blocker cuts off the upfield path, the slanter must play over the top of that blocker to maintain the pass rush lane and possibly contain.

- The looper, if it is the defensive end who is long sticking, must read the center. His long stick long should come as tight as possible to the slanter, thus creating a pick situation. If the center turns toward him with his far shoulder pointing up field, looper will attack that shoulder to maintain his pass rush lane. If the blocker sits flat to the line of scrimmage, the looper will bull rush that offensive lineman. If the blocker turns away, like zone pass protection, the looper will push off his near hip and rush vertically upfield. If an interior lineman is the looper, he will use the same technique as the looper in the two-man game.

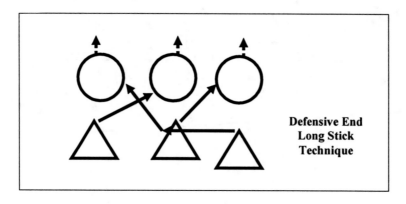

Defensive End
Long Stick
Technique

#87: Three-Man Delay Games

Objective: To teach a three-man delay stunt for attacking dropback pass and turnback protection

Equipment Needed: Ball on a stick

Description: This drill involves three offensive blockers and defensive lineman. On the snap of the ball on of the end, defensive lineman delays his slant by speed rushing up the field for three steps, planting the outside foot, then lateral shuffles and slams into the offensive blocker to the inside. If the end man is a slower interior lineman, he can use a turkey club move to shorten his steps. The next inside defensive lineman bull rushes the offensive lineman he is aligned on and then disengages him and breaks to the back of the next inside lineman. The looper takes one step toward the third offensive lineman and then loops (can use the long stick technique) behind the buttocks of both of the slanting defensive linemen. The looper will read the first offensive blocker and will react like any of the other two-man games. As a rule, if that gap is open, the looper should accelerate and come around the corner for the sack. Have players perform this drill with different three-man game combinations from the right and left sides. Do several repetitions of each.

Coaching Point: The sequence of individual stunts (e.g., who goes first second, third) should be assigned before the ball is snapped.

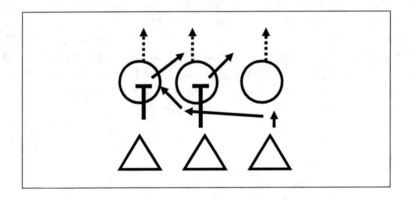

#88: Interior Rush vs. a Double-Team

Objective: To develop the defensive lineman's pass rush technique against a double-team

Equipment Needed: Ball on a stick

Description: For this drill, three offensive linemen are aligned side-by-side. The two defensive linemen align on the end men of the trio. The defenders will align head-up. The offensive blockers will execute a short, quick vertical set. The coach will stand behind the defensive linemen and signal the middle blocker on which side to double-team. On the snap of the ball, both defensive lineman explode forward out of their stance, maintaining low pad level, and jam both hands in the chest of the blocker they are aligned on. On the non-double-team side, the pass rusher will continue with a bull rush and use either the push-pull technique or slingshot technique to shed the blocker. On the double-team side, the middle blocker executes his short, quick vertical set first and then moves to double-team in the direction of the coach's signal. The defender should use his hands to bench press and bull rush through the double-team. The defensive lineman should keep his eyes on the quarterback to read the drop and passer arm action as he is driving the blockers back. He must not run around blocks to avoid the double-team. If the quarterback takes a short drop and cocks his arm in the throwing motion, the defender should get his hands up in the "eyesight lanes" (i.e., the lines of sight from the quarterback to his receivers with the opposite hand from the passer). Have players perform this drill with the double-teams coming from the right and left sides. Do several repetitions of each with different drops and arm actions by the quarterback.

Coaching Points:

- The defensive lineman being doubled-teamed must maintain his pass rush lane when splitting the blockers.
- If a defender feels he is pinned (i.e., if progress is stopped by the double-team), he should get his hand straight up (opposite hand of the quarterback's throwing arm) to obstruct the eyesight lane of the quarterback or to deflect the pass.
- The interior defensive linemen should get numerous repetitions versus the double-team on a daily basis.

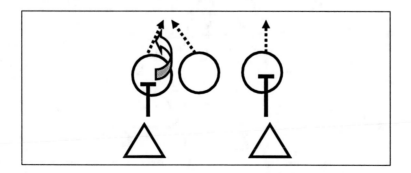

#89: 1-on-1 Team Pass Rush

Objective: To improve the defensive lineman's pass rush techniques and maintain his pass rush lane against a live offensive lineman

Equipment Needed: Football

Description: This drill will have five offensive linemen are aligned side-by-side and four defensive linemen. The defensive linemen will be aligned in either a 43 over or under scheme. Set up the drill on a yard-line marker and a pass rush grid (as shown in the diagram) to emphasize the defensive lineman's awareness to maintain his pass rush lane. The offensive blockers will use a short, quick vertical set on cadence. On ball movement from the center, all of the defensive linemen will get off explosively, work on their first three steps, and perform a hand parry while the offensive linemen are performing their punches. However, one pair of the offensive and defensive linemen will be live to the quarterback. The live pair is predetermined by the coach. If the defensive lineman is an end (an outside edge rusher), he will read the vertical set of the blocker and execute one of the appropriate moves for that type of vertical set. If the defensive lineman is an interior blocker, he can use a bull rush with one of the escape moves off of the power rush or use one of the foot counter moves. A free-standing bag, form-tackling dummy should be positioned at the quarterback spot so the defender has a landmark to rush the quarterback for a sack or practice stripping the football from the quarterback's hand. Have players perform this drill so that each player gets a few repetitions each from both sides of the ball.

Coaching Points:

- If the defensive lineman gets too deep on his pass rush, he should not get upfield behind the quarterback, but stop his rush by planting on his upfield foot, opening his hips toward the blocker, and running straight back to the line of scrimmage to reestablish his pass rush lane and contain the quarterback.
- To simulate a moving quarterback, the coach my substitute a player at the quarterback position. In this case, the defensive lineman should only tag the quarterback above the waist with two hands to limit injury.

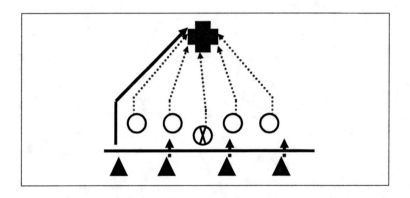

#90: Rush vs. Hinge—Turnback Protection

Objective: To improve the defensive lineman's pass rush techniques against the turnback and other hinge protections (These protections are primarily use on sprint or rollout offensive plays.)

Equipment Needed: Football or ball on a stick

Description: In this drill, three offensive linemen will align side-by-side while two defensive linemen will align on the two end men of the offensive line. All three blockers are given direction by the coach. The drill begins on ball movement. The coach, manager, or center can move the ball. On the snap of the ball, the blockers turn in the specified direction of the hinge-block technique. To hinge block, the blocker steps with the playside foot for one step and then drop-steps with his other foot. The action forms a wall of protection for the moving quarterback. The defensive lineman should take off on the snap and read the hinge block. Once the blocker turns, the defensive lineman should stop his attack, and use his backside arm to rip across the face of the playside blocker. He shouldn't take the bait and attempt to penetrate off the blocker's tail unless the gap is unnaturally large because of poor blocking technique. Have players perform this drill so that each player gets a few repetitions each with the hinges going to the right and left.

Coaching Points:

- The defensive linemen can also use a swipe escape technique to escape over the top of the blocker.
- To simulate a moving quarterback, the coach my substitute a player at the quarterback position. In this case, the defensive lineman should only tag the quarterback above the waist with two hands to limit injury.

#91: Rush vs. Slide Protection

Objective: To improve the defensive lineman's pass rush techniques against the slide protection

Equipment Needed: Football or ball on a stick

Description: In this drill, five offensive linemen will align side-by-side, one blocking back, a quarterback, while four defensive linemen align in either a 43 over or under scheme. Set up the drill on a yard-line marker, and establish a neutral zone. This aids the defensive linemen to read the slide protection and react according. All five blockers are given direction of the slide by the coach. The blocking back always goes opposite the slide direction. The drill begins on ball movement. The center will move the ball. On the snap of the ball, the blockers will slide on the line of scrimmage, and the back will attack the last defender on the line. To slide block, the blocker lateral shuffles three short power steps. This action forms a wall of protection for a dropback quarterback. The defensive linemen should take off on the snap and read the slide block. The defensive lineman attacks his original gap, works upfield, and maintains his pass rush lane. The defender should not chase the offensive lineman when he slides. The defensive end away from the slide must maintain contain on the quarterback and attack the running. That defensive end must handle a cut block from the blocking back. Have players perform this drill so that each player gets a few repetitions each with the slide protection going to the right and left.

Coaching Points:

- The defensive linemen must recognize the difference between slide protections (pass) and reach blocks (run). The techniques to defeat and escape those two types of blocks required different techniques.
- The defensive should not game plan twist games versus slide protection.
- To simulate the quarterback who steps up, the coach my substitute a player at the quarterback position. In this case, the defensive lineman should only tag the quarterback above the waist with two hands to limit injury.

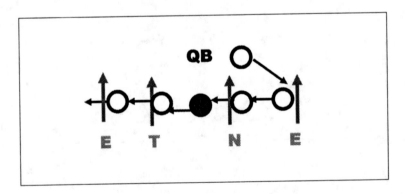

#92: 5-on-4 Read-and-React

Objective: To improve the defensive lineman's ability to read the type of pass protection and react with the proper pass rush techniques

Equipment Needed: Football, scout look cards (diagrams of the protection schemes)

Description: In this drill, five offensive linemen will align side-by-side, one blocking back, a quarterback, while four defensive linemen align in either a 43 over or under scheme. Set up the drill on a yard-line marker and establish a neutral zone. This aids the defensive linemen in reading the protection scheme, and reading and reacting accordingly. All the blockers and the quarterback are given the protection scheme by the coach, who is holding up large scheme cards while standing behind the defensive linemen. The quarterback will also see the type of pass drop (three- or five-step, sprint-out, bootleg). The schemes use are man/zone six-man protection, slide protection, turnback play-action, and bootleg (naked or guard pull). The drill begins on ball movement. The center will move the ball. On the snap of the ball, the blockers execute the protection called, and the quarterback executes the type of drop. The defensive linemen should explode of the ball on the snap and read the type of protection scheme and block. The defensive linemen will perform the proper techniques that match the type of pass protection set utilized by the offensive blockers. The defensive linemen will use the appropriate escape to shed the blocker. The defensive lineman will accelerate to the quarterback but should only tag the quarterback above the waist with two hands to limit injury. Have players perform this drill at least once a week, having the defensive linemen getting numerous repetitions based on the offensive protection schemes for that opponent.

Coaching Points:

- This drill enhances a defensive lineman's ability to rush the passer more effectively by recognizing the difference types of protection schemes. This will lower the reaction time, making the pass rush quicker and putting more pressure on the blocker to protect his quarterback.
- The coach can plan to add twist games if man/zone protections schemes are being used.

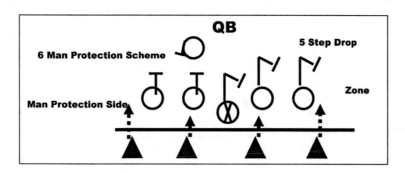

#93: Ultimate Effort

Objective: To improve the ability of defensive linemen to chase the football after it has been thrown

Equipment Needed: Football, lined field

Description: The defensive front is aligned in its positions. On the snap of the ball, the defenders rush the football. The defensive linemen can use a pass rush move or foot counter on air to stimulate a pass rush move. The coach simulates the actions of the quarterback by taking a five-step drop or aligned in a shotgun formation. Once the linemen are accelerating to the quarterback, the coach throws the ball to one of the four stationary receivers. These receivers can be 15 to 20 yards away. The defensive linemen plant their upfield foot, and sprint back to the line of scrimmage. Then, the closest defender will run to the spot of throw until the other defensive linemen get to the ball. All of the defensive lineman should then break down and sprint off the field. The coach should throw the ball to all receivers at least once in the drill.

Coaching Points:

- Each defensive lineman should keep his hands up to block the view of the quarterback (coach) once he completes his pass rush move on air.
- Once the ball has been thrown, each lineman should turn to chase the football, all the while visualizing stripping the receiver from behind.

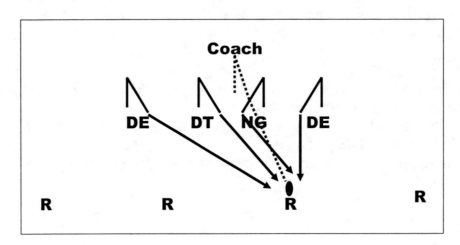

#94: Defending the Cutter

Objective: To improve the ability of defensive linemen to handle and play off cut blocks while rushing the quarterback who is sprinting out

Equipment Needed: Two free standing tackling dummies, football

Description: Place two free standing tackling dummies between three players who are in a four-point stance. The two outside players will be positioned two yards off of the line of scrimmage. One player, acting as a quarterback, will be in the backfield about seven yards ready to sprint out to the right or left. This drill should be performed on a yard-line marker. The coach will signal to the quarterback in which direction the quarterback should sprint out prior to the drill commencing. Two defensive linemen align in front of the two free-standing tackling dummies. On the snap of the ball, the defenders get off quickly, lead with their hands, and jam with two hands with low pad level and run their feet. Once the defenders have jammed the first bag and driven it back one yard, the quarterback sprints out laterally to the called side. The defensive linemen swipe off the tall dummies, laterally moving down the line. As the defenders move down the line, the players in a four-point stance will fire out and perform a cut block. The defender will lead with his hands, maintain low pad level, and jam his hands into the top front portion of the cutter's shoulder pads. As contact is being made, the defenders feet need to sprawl backwards so that the cutter cannot tie up the defensive lineman's legs. The defensive lineman closest to the quarterback will use an inside-out rush lane to the quarterback. The second defensive lineman will work down the line of scrimmage and maintain a proper pursuit angle. The defensive linemen pursue the quarterback until he is herded in and is two hands touched. Have players perform this drill in both directions.

Coaching Point: The coach must emphasize to each defensive lineman that he should not be moving forward on the cut block. Kicking their feet back and keeping pressure with the hands and arms on the cutter's shoulder pad will negate the cut and any further reblocking.

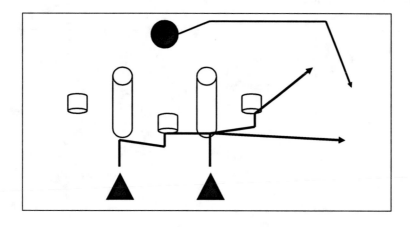

#95: Two-Level Pass Rush

Objective: To improve the ability of defensive linemen to encounter more than one blocker in route to the passer

Equipment Needed: Two agility bags or rubber strips, free standing tackling dummy with arms, ball on a stick

Description: Place two agility bags to mark a pass rush lane. Align a defensive lineman on an outside shade of an offensive blocker. Inside the offensive lineman is blocking back aligned seven yards from the line of scrimmage. To the inside of the blocking back will be a tall bag with arms to simulate the quarterback. Set up this drill on yard-line markers, and establish a neutral zone. The offensive lineman will vertical set with one of the three types of sets discussed prior. The offensive lineman will quickly set but only give light pressure when punching. This is so the defensive lineman can use a pass rush move and get to the second level of the blocking scheme. On ball movement, the defensive lineman will get off and execute a proper pass rush move and escape. Once the defender clears the first blocker, the blocking back will move to block the defensive lineman. Once again, the defensive lineman must utilize a sound and effective pass rush move to get by the blocking block. Once the defender is clear of the blocking back, he will accelerate to the quarterback and either tackle the dummy or perform a proper strip technique on the arm of the quarterback. Have players perform this drill in both directions.

Coaching Points:

- If an interior defensive lineman is executing this drill, the offensive lineman should execute a short, vertical set. The defensive lineman will execute either a bull rush with one of the two escapes or one of the two foot counter moves.
- The blocking back can stay high and block, or use a cut block on the rushing lineman.
- To simulate a quarterback that is throwing the ball, the coach my substitute a player at the quarterback position. As the defensive lineman is rushing, the quarterback will drop back and release the ball. The defensive lineman will perform a proper battered ball technique.

#96: Tracking Down the Screen

Objective: To improve the ability of defensive linemen to get off the ball, enhance low pad level, and redirecting to pursue a screen or flair pass

Equipment Needed: Two agility bags or rubber strips, five free standing tackling dummy with arms, ball on a stick

Description: Align the dummies as shown in the diagram. This drill needs to be performed on a yard-line marker and established neutral zone. Two defensive linemen align on an outside shade of the tandem dummies. The tandem dummies are a placed three yards apart from each other in a straight line. The tandem dummies simulate a firm deflect vertical set. The distance between the bags emphasizes that a pass move must be completed with four yards of the line of scrimmage. A pass rush lane is created between the rubber strips and the tandem dummies. On ball movement, the defensive linemen will get off and execute a speed rush move with a dip-and-rip escape. Once the defender clears the last of the tandem dummies blocking back, the defenders will accelerate to the quarterback bag that is set up for each defender. The defender will now redirect around the bag and sprint to running back, catching the screen or flair pass. Have players perform this drill in both directions.

Coaching Point: Variety can be added to the drill by pairing up the defensive linemen to make it a competition drill.

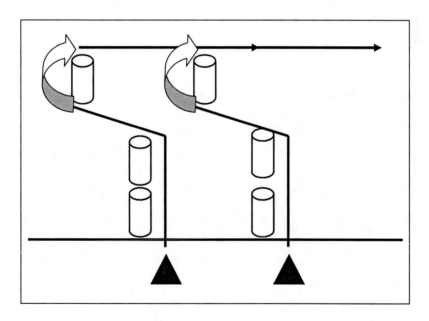

11

Tackling, Ball Disruption, and Team Pursuit: Basic Fundamentals Development for Defensive Linemen

#97: "Big Five" Tackling

Objective: To teach defenders how to tackle properly with emphasis on safety

Equipment Needed: Shield, agility bags or rubber strips, cones or dots.

Description: Defenders must utilize a proper fit position that emphasizes safety when tackling. The basic components of a sound and effective tackle are that the eyes and head must be up, with shoulders square to the player being tackled. The defender should club both arms violently, keeping the elbows rubbing the ballcarrier's ribs. The tackle must maintain the power angles at the ankles, knees, and hips by keeping them bent during the entire tackling process. The basic tackling drills are as follows:

- Form fit: Two defenders pair up and face each other in a two-point stance. One defender will be the offensive ballcarrier and will raise his arms laterally to shoulder height. The defender who will be tackler will align on the edge of the offensive player not more than 12 inches away. The tackler will bend his ankles, knees, and hips to create the power angles. On the "go" command given by the coach, the tackler will step with his inside foot into the ballcarrier's crotch, shoot his arms violently upward (club), keep his shoulders squared and head and eyes while stepping with the outside foot six inches. The tackler will repeat this process continuously for three repetitions. The tackler will reset on the opposite edge and repeat the three reps when the coach gives the "go" command.

- Club and base: The drill will be set up just like the form fit drill except the tackler and the ballcarrier will be one to two yards apart. The ballcarriers will hold shields. The defenders will align on the opposite edge of the ballcarrier from where the tackle will be taking place. The tackles will begin the drill in an athletic stance. On the "go" command, the tackler will accelerate to the shield and perform the proper techniques as described in the form fit drill. Once the tackle has occurred, the coach will reset the tacklers and perform the drill for two more repetitions. Then, that group of defensive linemen will switch sides and perform another three repetitions.

- Rapid fire: Two defenders pair up, once again, in athletic stances, at each end of an agility bag or rubber strip. The ballcarrier will hold a shield. The coach will signal which direction the ballcarrier should run first. On the "go" command, the ballcarrier will run to one side of the agility bag, while the tackler will attack and tackle the ballcarrier using the principles outlined. Immediately after the tackle, the ballcarrier retreats (as does the tackler) to the end of the bag and repeats the drill to the opposite side. This process goes on for six repetitions, three for each side.

- Angle: Pair up two players, in a five-yard square marked off with cones or dots, in a two-point stance. The players will line up in the middle of the cones (dots) five yards apart. On the "go" command, the defensive lineman will activate his feet with quick chops, slowly advancing forward (shimmy technique), reading the cut by the ballcarrier. The designated ballcarrier, without a fake, runs three-quarter speed directly to one of the far cones on a diagonal. The defender tackles the ballcarrier on an angle. The defender must make contact with his eyes and head up in front of the ballcarrier, clubbing violently with his arms and getting both feet in front of the ballcarrier's body.
- Angle spin: This drill is executed the same way as the angle tacking drill. The only change will be that when the tackler clubs the ballcarrier, the ballcarrier will spin toward the inside to escape the tackle.

Coaching Point: The basic tackling techniques ensure that the tackler's whole body absorbs the contact—not just one area, which can result in injury.

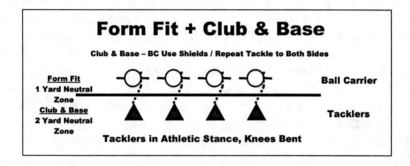

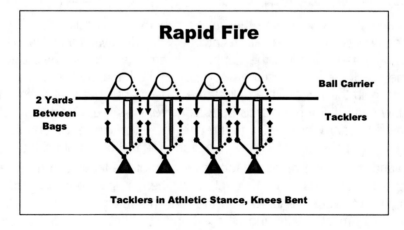

#98: Ball Disruption and Scoring

Objective: To increase the opportunities by defensive linemen to create turnovers by developing sound and effective techniques to that create fumbles and aid in recovering the ball/scoring

Equipment Needed: Shield, agility bags or rubber strips, cones, or dots, ball on a stick

Description: In order to implement this ball disruption attitude with the defensive linemen, a few strategies must be considered. Drill the techniques every week. Work pursuit drills with all players going for the ball. Teach them to be in position to take advantage of a caused fumble. Set goals and rewards. Have a turnover takeaway circuit every week.

- Tomahawk and punch: If there is no space between the ballcarrier's body and his triceps, meaning you can't see the ball from the back, or if he is swinging his arm, you want to bring down the hammer down and use a tomahawk technique. Position the ballcarrier and defender front-to-back one yard apart from each other. On the "go" command, the ballcarrier (with football in arm) carries it as described for the drill. The ballcarrier commences running at three-quarter speed, and the defensive lineman chases him. When there is no space between him and the ballcarrier, the defensive lineman will grab the shoulder pad with the away hand, violently yank the ballcarrier back, and strike down on the top of the ball (tomahawk), nearer to his fingers, with a closed fist. He should secure the away hand over or around the shoulder to grab the jersey on the ballcarrier's chest. He should try to straighten his ball arm to his side so he can't secure it. The defender should always run the feet and never be dead weight. Have players perform the drill from both sides.
- Punch-and-rip: If you can see the ball from behind, it is called "turtle head." The defender wants to use a similar technique with the away hand (as in tomahawk and punch). But this time, the defensive lineman will throw a violent upper cut into the ball. If the ball doesn't dislodge, open the hand, he should twist the palm outward, grab the front of the ball by the ballcarrier's fingers, and violently rip his arm down and pull it behind his back as he runs his feet. Teach the defender to ride the ballcarrier's facemask into the turf. The entire maneuver should be as fast and violent as possible. Have players perform the drill from both sides.
- Scoop-and-score: First, place the football on top of the tackling dummy, essentially making the football its head. The defensive linemen line up a few yards from the dummy in a three-point stance. On the movement key (ball on a stick), the first player in line must charge and hit the dummy, knocking the ball to the ground.

Next, the player must run to the football, grab it with two hands, bending his ankles, knees, and hips, and run toward the end zone. In another variation of the drill, the player can simply fall on the football after it is knocked free. Sometimes, defensive players get too caught up in gathering a fumble and returning it for a touchdown, and they never recover the fumble to begin with. This version of the football drill can help to alleviate that tendency.

- Rolling ball scoop-and-score: The defender will align five yards away from the coach. On coach's command, the defender will run at the coach. The coach will roll the ball at the feet of the defensive lineman. The defender must bend at the ankles, knees, and hips, scoop the ball up, and run past the coach. The coach must make sure that the defender tucks the ball away.

Coaching Point: If your defensive players perfect the ball disruption and scoop-and-score drills, it might make them more comfortable going after the ball the next time it pops free—and it might help you win the turnover battle against your opponent.

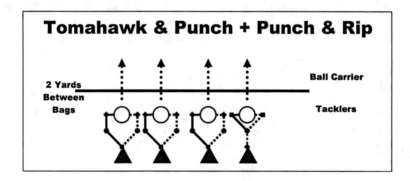

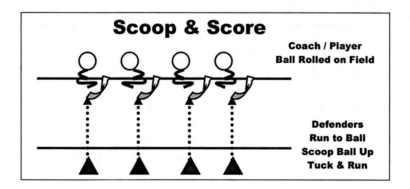

#99: Run Rabbit

Objective: To develop a defensive lineman's fundamental skill of defensive pursuit (taking the proper angle of pursuit) and setting the tempo to be an effective defensive unit with an intense, all-out effort that is driven by an insatiable desire to get to the football and to put the ballcarrier on the ground

Equipment Needed: Football, ball on a stick

Description: The defense unit is aligned in the middle of the field on a yard-line marker, maintaining a neutral zone. Each defensive linemen has an offensive linemen paired up with him. The defensive line coach will stand behind the linebackers and give a direction to the offensive linemen. This direction will indicate which way the offensive linemen will use a reach block on the charging defenders. In the backfield will be the defensive coordinator as well as two running backs (flanking aligned on hashes). On ball movement, the defensive linemen attack the offensive linemen who are carrying out their reach block. The defensive linemen will use their push-pull technique and

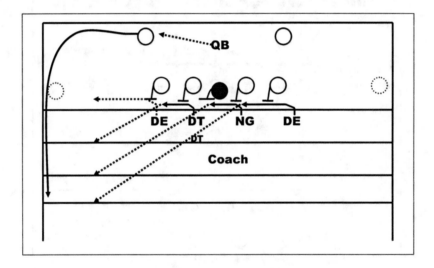

proper escapes techniques (rip, swipe, and shrug) to shed the blockers. Also, the coach will pitch the ball to the right or left to one of the running backs who then run wide getting to the corner and turning upfield down the sideline. The rest of the defensive players will do an up-down and then join in with the pursuit. All defenders take a pursuit angle to cut off the ballcarrier. No defensive player should follow the same color jersey as they pursue. The defensive end closest to the ballcarrier will sprint straight down the line of scrimmage. The next defensive lineman (interior ballside) will sprint to where the end originally aligned and then take a pursuit angle with keeps him five yards upfield from the defensive end. The other two defensive linemen play down the line to the next inside defensive lineman's original alignment and then take on the five yards from the previous defensive lineman's pursuit angle. Each defender should take an angle that allows him to tag the offensive player on the shoulder. Each defensive position coach is directed to judge the stance, technique, pursuit angle, and effort of his players. If any player fails to rate acceptable in any of the categories, the repetition does not count. The defensive coordinator sets the number of perfect plays each day. Have players perform the drill so that each group has to pursue in both directions.

Coaching Points:

- Variation on the drill is that the offensive coach use two wide receivers plus the two running backs. The defensive coordinator can throw a bullet pass to one of the receivers near the sideline.
- The drill can be an excellence exercise because it teaches defensive players to realize that they have to not only be responsible for themselves, but also to each other.
- The coaches should not give advice or warnings to the defensive players. Once the objective of the drill and the expectations are explained, the players should learn from their mistakes.

#100: Attacking the Offensive Schemes

Objective: To develop the ability of the defensive linemen, linebackers and safeties to read/react and properly fit their opponent's run and play-action blocking schemes

Equipment Needed: Football, large scout cards (diagramed plays)

Description: The defense unit is aligned in the middle of the field on a yard-line marker, maintaining a neutral zone. The defensive unit consists of four defensive linemen, three linebackers, and defensive backs that align in a two-deep scheme. The offensive unit will have all players but without wide receivers. On offense, the opponent's top-five run plays and the top-three play-action schemes will be worked on. These plays should be scripted and drawn on large scout cards so that the drill can be run efficiently and effectively. The defensive unit should show all of the fronts, stunts, and blitzes that will be used based on game plan. On ball movement, the offensive unit should executer their assignments and the defensive unit will attack with proper reads. This drill should be performed full speed to the timing down. A quick whistle must be used. This drill is about assignments and timing; it is not a tackling drill.

Coaching Point: The coach should make sure that all defenders are taking on the blocks with proper shoulder and arm techniques to maintain leverage on the ball carrier and execute the spill principle.

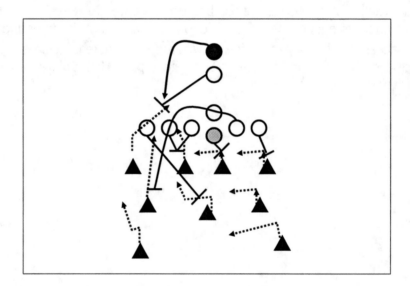

#101: Stop the Score

Objective: To develop the defensive lineman's ability to use proper techniques to defend against an opponent's goal-line attack at full speed

Equipment Needed: Football, large scout cards (diagramed plays)

Description: The drill is usually structured according to a script. An offensive coach shows the offensive unit an alignment card that details their assignments in the goal-line attack. The quarterback calls the play and the snap count. The offensive line then sprints to the line of scrimmage. The defensive unit is in its called alignment and makes adjustments according to the formation. The play is executed, the whistle is sounded, and the offensive players sprint back to the huddle. The defensive returns quickly to their pre-assignment alignments. The coaches should do their coaching as the players return back for the next play. Once the offense returns to the huddle, another card is immediately shown. The sequence repeats until the script for that defensive unit has been completed (seven plays). If possible, two offensive units should be employed. The defenders should not be allowed to put the ballcarrier on the ground since defenders must be trained to knock the ballcarrier back and take pride in the challenge of stopping the opponent. The ball should be spotted as by a defensive coach according to the script.

Coaching Points:

- The two interior defensive linemen (tackle, nose) will be in a four-point stance. They will align off the ball, depending how far the ball is from the goal line. If the ball is two to three yards away, the two interior defensive linemen align on the side leg of the guards. If the ball is one to two yards away, the two line up in the gap between the guards and the center. If the ball is inside one yard, they both align on the outside leg of the center. In all cases, on ball movement they will crawl on all fours quickly into the backfield. If they clear the blockers, then they can rise and pursue the ball flat down the line.

- The two exterior defensive linemen (ends) will align in a tight five on the tackle. They can be in a three- or four-point stance. They both will get off the ball and drive through the neck of the offensive tackle. Maintaining low pad level is a must for these defensive ends.

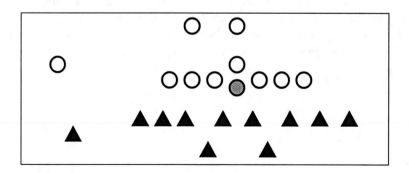

About the Author

Mike Cieri is a coaching veteran of 35 college seasons and 42 campaigns overall, including being a high school head coach. Cieri is the defensive line coach and special teams coordinator for the 10th winningest Division III football program in the country: Montclair State University. As the run coordinator at MSU, Cieri has helped the Red Hawk defensive line to be #1 in rush defense seven times in the last 12 seasons, and his defensive lines have led the New Jersey Athletic Conference with the most quarterback sacks (77) and 58 battered passes over that same time period. During that same time span, MSU has won three NJAC championships and appeared in five post-seasons, including three NCAA Division III plays reaching the Sweet 16 and an ECAC championship. Since 2003, at least one member of the defensive line has been represented on the NJAC All-Conference Team. At the present time, one of Cieri's defensive linemen is a highly rated prospect for the New York Giants.

Prior to Cieri's tenure at Montclair State, he spent 19 seasons at Fairleigh-Dickinson University Florham as an offensive, defensive, and special teams coordinator. While at FDU, the defensive units rose from the bottom of the Middle Atlantic Conference to a nationally-ranked defensive in 1999. In addition, the offense set several school and MAC records.

Over the last several years, Cieri has regularly been a speaker at various clinics and conventions. He presented special teams topics at the AFCA Buzz sessions in 2011 and 2012, and he has spoken the past five years as a Glazier clinician on both defensive line play and special teams. Cieri also traveled to the Washington State Football Coaches Clinic to present various topics on defensive line play, run fits from the 43 defense, subgrouping packages, and zone blitzing out of the base 43 and dime packages.

Cieri has authored several articles. His most recent article appeared in the January/February 2014 issue of *This Is AFCA* entitled "Reinforcing Critical Punt Pressure Skills." In addition, Cieri has published three articles in *American Football Monthly*, and recently author the book *101 Winning Special Teams and Defensive Line Drills* for Coaches Choice. Also, Cieri has produced 13 DVDs on special teams and defensive line play (also available through Coaches Choice).